ARTIFICIAL INTELLIGENCE METHODS FOR OPTIMIZATION OF THE SOFTWARE TESTING PROCESS

Uncertainty, Computational Techniques, and Decision Intelligence Book Series

Series Editors

Tofigh Allahviranloo, PhD
Faculty of Engineering and Natural Sciences, Istinye University, Istanbul, Turkey

Narsis A. Kiani, PhD
Algorithmic Dynamics Lab, Department of Oncology-Pathology & Center of Molecular Medicine, Karolinska Institute, Stockholm, Sweden

Witold Pedrycz, PhD
Department of Electrical and Computer Engineering, University of Alberta, Canada

For more information about the UCTDI series, please visit: https://www.elsevier.com/books-and-journals/book-series/uncertainty-computational-techniques-and-decision-intelligence

ARTIFICIAL INTELLIGENCE METHODS FOR OPTIMIZATION OF THE SOFTWARE TESTING PROCESS

With Practical Examples and Exercises

SAHAR TAHVILI
Product Development Unit, Cloud RAN, Integration and Test
Ericsson AB, Stockholm, Sweden

Division of Product Realisation
School of Innovation, Design and Engineering
Mälardalen University, Eskilstuna, Sweden

LEO HATVANI
Division of Product Realisation
School of Innovation, Design and Engineering
Mälardalen University, Eskilstuna, Sweden

ACADEMIC PRESS
An imprint of Elsevier

ELSEVIER

ISBN: 978-0-323-91913-5

For information on all Academic Press publications
visit our website at https://www.elsevier.com/books-and-journals

Publisher: Mara Conner
Editorial Project Manager: John Leonard
Production Project Manager: Swapna Srinivasan
Designer: Mark Rogers

Typeset by VTeX

Working together
to grow libraries in
developing countries

www.elsevier.com • www.bookaid.org

I would like to dedicate this book to my sister Sara and my niece Nilsa, who have always stood by me every step of the way with unconditional love and support.

– Sahar

I would like to dedicate this book to my parents who have always encouraged me on my science journeys.

– Leo

Contents

List of figures

List of tables

Biography

Sahar Tahvili is an operations team leader in the product development unit, Cloud RAN, integration and test at Ericsson AB, and also a researcher at Mälardalen University, Sweden. Sahar holds a PhD in software engineering; her doctoral thesis entitled "Multi-Criteria Optimization of System Integration Testing" was named one of the best new Software Integration Testing books by BookAuthority. She earned her BS and MS degrees in Applied Mathematics with an emphasis on optimization. Sahar's research focuses on artificial intelligence, advanced methods for testing complex software-intensive systems, and designing decision support systems (DSSs). Previously she worked as a senior researcher at the Research Institutes of Sweden and as a senior data scientist at Ericsson AB.

Leo Hatvani is a lecturer at Mälardalen University, Sweden. Leo holds a Licentiate degree in the verification of embedded systems from Mälardalen University. His current research focuses on artificial intelligence and advanced methods for testing complex software-intensive systems. His teaching is focused on improving Industry 4.0 production processes and product development by integrating artificial intelligence and augmented and virtual reality. He is working closely with Mälardalen Industrial Technology Centre (MITC), which cooperates with a number of regional companies to introduce Industry 4.0 practices into the Swedish industry.

Preface

The story of writing this book started after we tried to conclude our research in the fields of artificial intelligence and software testing. From 2015 to 2020, we published our research results in several conferences, journals, and also Sahar's PhD thesis. Then it was time to move on to the next chapter in our careers. But we found ourselves seeking out a conclusion to this research.

During this time we changed homes, cities, domains, and jobs, the coronavirus outbreak started, and our homes became our offices, but our research always stayed with us. We were always on the lookout for the next step of our research. How we can find some new use cases? Is this research applicable in other domains? How can we facilitate the testing effort in today's technology?

We still remember our first days in the industry as young researchers with a heightened pressure to impress the testing team. The first time we went to the Bombardier Transportation offices in Västerås (the company's name changed to Alstom Sweden AB), we met the integration testing team and they showed us a comprehensive presentation about the testing process. We found out how different real-world industrial software testing can be from the theoretical descriptions and toy examples used in academia.

At that time, many concepts were unclear to us. Either due to our lack of knowledge in the testing domain or the slight differences between theory and practice. We still remember the complexity of the test configuration figures, traceability matrix, testing pipelines, and numerous acronyms. We did not even know from which point we should start. However, we trusted in the process and that "hard work will pay off." Then we started from scratch.

After some time, we began to understand the testing process in the industry. Also, the testing team began to understand our intentions and ideas. During our research, we did not just focus on different artificial intelligence-based solutions; we also developed a common understanding between us and the stakeholders in the industry.

Within our daily close collaboration with engineers and testing teams at Alstom Sweden AB and Ericsson AB, we realized that there is potential and need for our research. On the other hand, continuously learning from the testing experts pushed our limits and forced us out of our comfort zones.

Finally, we are here now, presenting our book, discussing our experiences, and sharing our challenges and discoveries with the readers. This book is a beginning of a story, not just about artificial intelligence applications in the software testing domain, but also about overcoming the weak points, fears, and restrictions by not giving up, asking questions, and always learning. We are still at the beginning of an endless learning process. Support us and each other to be better; each one of us can make a difference. Together we can make a massive change in both science and the world.

Acknowledgments

Our sincere thanks go to Pontus Östling, Gunnar le Grand, Dr. Sigrid Eldh, Yulin Cui, Cristina Landin, and Anders Caspar at Ericsson AB, who have invested their valuable time and always been supportive to us throughout the work on this book.

We would like to express our sincere gratitude to the integration testing teams at Alstom Sweden AB for their patience, motivation, and immense knowledge. A very special thank you goes to Dr. Ola Sellin and Henrik Jonsson at Alstom Sweden AB for their support during the research that built the foundation of this book.

Our deepest gratitude goes to our families, friends, and also our colleagues: Dr. Nima Dokoohaki, Jonas Österberg, Dr. Hessam Shadman, Dr. Anita Simhag, Iraj Mesdaghi, Professor Markus Bohlin, and Shahab Darvish, who have always been there for us. Without them, we could have never reached this far.

Sahar Tahvili and Leo Hatvani

Stockholm
June 2022

Software testing, artificial intelligence, decision intelligence, and test optimization

## CHAPTER ONE

Introduction

"Learning is a profoundly important part of what makes us human. It is also something good old-fashioned artificial intelligence struggled with."

Luke Dormehl

1.1. Our digital era for a better future

Nowadays, not a single day goes by without receiving news about the digital world. We are somehow surrounded by social media, algorithms, cryptocurrencies, cyber–attacks, and artificial intelligence. In fact, we are in an age of rapid technological progress, although some of the news about our digital world and advanced technologies is still fiction and wishes. Despite all the progress and positive effects of the digital era, we are still struggling to handle and be prepared for unforeseen global risks. Monitoring the impact of the COVID–19 pandemic on our daily lives, mental health, and economy is a good example of evaluating our capabilities and today's technologies. However, even with modern technology, some unforeseen events happen due to software glitches. The big demand for new devices and applications, competitors, and market share can directly impact the quality of new technologies. While the technology's demand is continuously empowering the enterprises, numerous records of cheating in the test process are reported. Sometimes paying no attention to the test result and product quality can cause a penalty of millions of dollars, and a single overtly minuscule bug in an aircraft system can cause a fatal crash. Additionally, today's technology is in danger of being overestimated, which might mislead consumers with respect to its capabilities and applications. For instance, when we discuss artificial intelligence today, it sounds like artificial intelligence is the cure for all diseases, which can easily be applied and implemented in different areas and save more and more lives. Well, this statement is both true and false.

Today's version of artificial intelligence mostly refers to a device or an application that can make decisions based on the received information like human intelligence. Artificial intelligence has a wide range of applications, from simple GPS navigation system to the control of COVID–19 and even recognizing cancerous tumors in computed tomography scans. The daily

Artificial Intelligence Methods for Optimization of the Software Testing Process
https://doi.org/10.1016/B978-0-32-391913-5.00012-9

wide and critical application of artificial intelligence makes it an important factor in computer science research and also a buzzword in the digital marketplace.

Adaptation of new artificial intelligence technologies in the software development process is still at its infancy level compared to self-driving or voice-assisted control systems. Although most tech companies are focusing more and more on artificial intelligence, the problem of data availability and lack of artificial intelligence explainability is still preventing new startups or even large industries from easily employing new artificial intelligence technologies. After spending several years working in industrial research in the software testing domain, we can conclude that explainable artificial intelligence is the most critical factor for implementing artificial intelligence in industries. Presenting artificial intelligence as a black box[1] learning system to industries can be a huge barrier to entry and growth. On the other hand, employing artificial intelligence as an assistive tool and engaging the testing team for improving the quality of the dataset has helped us to present a white box[2] version of artificial intelligence. Although increasing software quality and reducing the unpredictable risks is vital, still, the most demanded usage of artificial intelligence in the software testing domain is test automation. In fact, most enterprises are aiming to reduce the amount of mundane and tedious tasks in the testing process. During our research with several industries, we had the opportunity to show how employing artificial intelligence technologies at different stages of the software testing process can help enterprises to increase the quality of the software product and optimize the testing process.

1.2. What is in this book?

This book consists of two main parts. The first part provides an introduction to the overall work on the use of artificial intelligence, including challenges, issues, and needs, in the software testing domain. Chapter 2 explains the background of the software testing concept and its history. Chapter 3 focuses more on transformation, vectorization, and optimization. In Chapter 4 we review the history of text analytics and we analyze text

---

[1] In the context of this book, a black box is a system that can be viewed in terms of its inputs and outputs, and its exact inner function remains hidden.

[2] In contrast to the black box, white box systems can be fully inspected and their functionality can be observed.

transformation and representation, vectorization, machine learning, deep neural network models, and also imbalanced learning. The topic of decision intelligence, multi-criterion decision-making, and test optimization techniques are exhaustively discussed in Chapter 4.

The structure and pipeline of the proposed solutions for optimization of the testing process are depicted in Chapter 5. Moreover, several industrial case studies from Ericsson AB and Alstom Sweden AB are presented in Chapter 5, which are focused on the telecommunication and safety-critical systems domains, respectively. We also review some available methods for implementing the proposed solutions in Python in this chapter. Chapter 6 clarifies some points of test artifact vectorization benefits and also discusses some major barriers to artificial intelligence adoption in industries. Finally, Chapter 7 concludes this part by discussing the presented contributions.

The second part of this book is mainly focused on practical examples and Python exercises. It also offers an introduction to the Python language, the data sources, additional source codes, and the utilized ground truths and data collection and annotation methods.

Since all the provided optimization solutions in this book are exemplified by at least one industrial case study, this book can be used by testers, troubleshooters, and also test managers in the industries for reproducibility. Moreover, this book provides a solid background and structure for all the proposed solutions. As mentioned above, Part 2 provides some practical examples and Python exercises that can be utilized by advanced undergraduate and graduate students in mathematics, statistics, computer science, any engineering field, and operations research and as a reference for professionals.

1.2.1 What is in the practical examples and exercises?

Part 2 consists of two chapters. Chapter 8 provides all required information for the environment installation and packages. The intent of Chapter 9 is to provide some Python exercises for the readers. Moreover, all the exercises are mapped with the information and industrial cases studies in Chapter 5. Readers will learn about computational approaches for a range of challenges, including searching high-dimensional spaces, handling problems where there are multiple competing objectives, and accommodating uncertainty in the metrics. Figures, examples, and exercises convey the intuition behind the proposed solutions. The text provides concrete implementations in the Python programming language.

1.2.2 What you will need

The exercises in this book are designed with the programmers in mind. However, the readers are able to take their own ideas for solving the exercises. Please do not forget the role of curiosity in innovation; innovation happens where ideas flourish. At an early stage of our research, we worked on an industrial project with a great team but no data was available at that time. During our research, we learned how to overcome the obstacles that are holding our goals hostage! In this book, we share some of our experiences with the readers about how artificial intelligence can be applied step by step in industries and how we can overcome the barriers. Being humble and patient is key!

1.3. What is missing?

This book is mainly about the application of different artificial intelligence models, e.g., machine learning, deep learning, and natural language processing, with a focus on test optimization. This book is written at an intermediate to advanced level for master level students and also software testing experts in industries. Moreover, we aimed to design this book to be comprehensive, where the proposed optimization solutions can be employed in other domains such as social media analytics. In this regard, we have included certain topics and subjects and excluded others. Our main criteria to select a topic were applicability and reproducibility. Therefore, a few subjects were omitted because they did not fit within the overall structure of this book. Although we are tried to address the problem of industrial large datasets, the proposed solutions in this book might not be sufficient for solving big data problems such as accumulating data from different sources.

CHAPTER TWO

Basic software testing concepts

Chapter points

- This chapter provides background information on the basic concepts and preliminaries in the area of software development.
- Comprehensive background information on software testing is provided.
- Several industrial examples of test artifacts are given.
- A brief history of software testing is provided.
- A brief overview of the conducted research on the application of artificial intelligence in the software testing domain is presented.

"Verification: Are we building the product right?
Validation: Are we building the right product?"

Barry Boehm

2.1. Software development life cycle

Even though the question *"What is software testing?"* may result in multiple answers, for the moment no one can doubt that software testing is an important and valuable phase in the software development life cycle.

The process of software testing has two main missions. First, one must evaluate the functionality of a software application to check whether the developed software meets the specified requirements [1]. Second, to ensure quality, one must strive to identify the defects to ensure that the product is bug-free. Software testing can also be considered as an investigation into the quality perspectives of both software products and services. Since software testing can interact with other phases of the software development life cycle, it can also be considered as the risk identification process in the software implementation phase.

Before diving into the process of software testing, its benefits, and the interaction with other development phases, it is important to understand what the term *"software development life cycle"* means.

Definition 2.1. The software development life cycle is a process that aims to design, develop, and test a software product [2].

Artificial Intelligence Methods for Optimization of
the Software Testing Process
https://doi.org/10.1016/B978-0-32-391913-5.00013-0

The software development life cycle can mainly be divided into three main activities: *design*, *development*, and *evaluation*. Each of the mentioned activities can be further divided into several phases or steps. Fig. 2.1 shows a customized version of a software development life cycle provided by us through monitoring different software development life cycle processes at several Swedish companies.

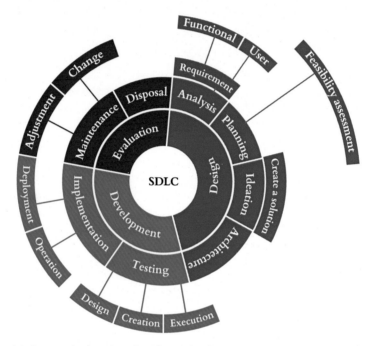

Figure 2.1 A customized version of a software development life cycle (SDLC). Source: Authors' own contribution, inspired by the original model of the software development life cycle.

As highlighted in Fig. 2.1, to complete each main step, several activities need to be done. Moreover, the customized version of the software development life cycle process in Fig. 2.1 is also mapped with a DevOps model. Generally, a DevOps model is a combination of cultural philosophies, practices, and tools that increase a company's ability to deliver applications or services at high velocity [3]. The main goal of employing the DevOps model is to improve products at a faster pace compared to the traditional software development and also infrastructure management processes [4]. The following paragraph provides distilled information regarding each step for the provided customized version of the software development life cycle in Fig. 2.1.

1. **Design.** During the design phase, several parameters such as stakeholder requirements, business rules, project planning, process diagrams, and technical architectures need to be analyzed. In this regard, the design phase can be done by performing the following activities:

   - **Analysis.** Generally, analysis refers to the requirement analysis which aims to capture all details of each requirement and analyze how each requirement is going to be satisfied. Moreover, the requirements also can be grouped into user (also known as non-functional requirements) and functional requirements. The user requirement explains the client requirements for the system [5], whereas a functional requirement describes a particular service that must be offered when certain conditions are met [6]. In this step, the stakeholders discuss both mentioned requirements of the software that needs to be developed.

   - **Planning.** Planning can be considered as a fundamental process of realizing a software program should be built [7]. Additionally, in the planning step, the feasibility of technical ideas, business, and organization should be assessed. The result of the feasibility assessment needs to be approved later by the steering committee to make sure the project supports business goals and objectives.

   - **Ideation.** When the team has a common idea of the requirements and the software project's foundations, a proper solution needs to be created that satisfies customers' needs, requirements, and also expectations [8]. However, in the ideation process, besides generating a broad set of ideas, some unexpected needs that are not anticipated before should be considered.

   - **Architecture.** Architecture illustrates a blueprint for a software system, which describes a structured solution, the major components, and also the interactions among species at each component. Furthermore, some common quality attributes such as performance and security need to be analyzed and optimized in this step [9]. The architecture step also includes a set of significant decisions related to software development that should be aligned with the business objectives and the organization.

2. **Development.** The development phase can mainly be grouped into implementation and testing steps. The main goal of the development phase is to implement a formal and organizational information system based on the designed prototype in the design phase [10]. If the information system addresses all functional and user requirements it will enter the testing phase.

- **Implementation.** After all mentioned design activities are completed, developers start implementation according to the requirements and design to develop a rough prototype of the software product (see the "Deployment" step in Fig. 2.1). Moreover, the required policies, guidelines, procedures, and standards for the implementation step are defined by the stakeholders. The implementation step usually includes the following operational activities: creation of a database for gathering the relevant data and creation of a graphical user interface which can interact with the backend [11].

- **Testing.** Testing can be considered as the most critical step in the development phase. The main objective of this step is to ensure that all requirements are met. In this regard, the components and their interactions should be tested. The testing step can be divided into the following three main activities: test design, test creation, and test execution. In the test design and creation steps, the requirements (both functional and non-functional) need to be analyzed in order to create a specific test case. Later, the created test cases will be executed generally into the following main testing levels: system testing, integration testing, acceptance testing, and unit testing [1].

3. **Evaluation.** During this step, one aims to deploy the system while identifying the system weaknesses [12]. Although the evaluation is the final phase of the software development life cycle, in an agile process evaluation should take place during all the mentioned phases. Moreover, the following two main decisions can be made based on the evaluation process.

- **Maintenance.** Maintenance involves making changes in hardware and software and also making adjustments to requirements and policies to improve the system's performance [13]. Additionally, enhanced security, identification of unanticipated needs, and addressing of user requirements can be achieved in this step.

- **Disposal.** Disposal represents the end of the software development life cycle when the system in question is no longer useful, needed, or relevant [13]. Based on the decisions in this step, the information system might be discarded, destroyed, or archived, or all arrangements may need to be transmitted to a new system.

We need to consider that the mentioned phases, steps, and activities can be changed, skipped, or merged in different software development life cycles. Consequently, the provided information in Fig. 2.1 is mapped and transferred from some large-scale software development projects which are going to be analyzed as case studies in the upcoming chapters.

2.2. Software testing

As stated in Section 2.1, software testing can be considered as the most vital step in the software development life cycle. The main objective of testing is to ensure the highest possible quality in the final product in order to avoid a faulty product being delivered to the end-user. The lack of adequate quality assurance might cause a loss of confidence in the company, a bad reputation, or penalties worth millions of dollars. As is obvious now, software testing is a complex process; therefore, testing a software product is a time- and resource-consuming process which can take up to 50% of the total development cost [14]. ANSI/IEEE 1059 standard defines the software testing process as follows [15].

Definition 2.2. Software testing is a process of analyzing a software item to detect the differences between existing and required conditions and to evaluate the features of the software item.

In other words, software testing aims to check whether the actual software product meets the expected (functional and user) requirements and to ensure that the final software product is defect-free.

2.2.1 The procedure of software testing

Today, the process of testing a software product can be performed manually, semi-automatically, and fully automatically, which all relate to the procedure of executing a test case.

Definition 2.3. A test case is a specification of the inputs, the execution's pre-conditions and post-conditions, the testing procedure, and also the expected results which need to be analyzed in order to verify compliance with a specific requirement [16].

In manual testing, a tester performs the tests step by step following a test case (specification), whereas during automated testing, a test case (script) is executed by employing test automation tools and frameworks. As the name suggests, semi-automated testing is a combination of manual and automated testing procedures, where there are some limitations to automating the entire testing process or advantages to keeping segments of the process

Table 2.1 Comparison of automated and manual software testing in six aspects.

Parameter	Manual testing	Automated testing
Test design	Does not require the coding process.	Drives a test-driven development design.
Setup	Requires a more straightforward test execution and system setup.	Requires less complex test execution and system setup.
Processing time	Time-consuming and requires human resources and observation. It has a higher risk of missing out on the pre-decided test deadline.	Significantly faster than manual testing, does not require human judgment and observation. Also, it has a lower risk of missing out on a pre-decided deadline.
Cost	Not cost-efficient for a large product with a high volume of test cases.	Not cost-efficient for a small-size product with a low volume of test cases.
Accuracy	Has a lower accuracy due to the possibility of bias and error in the human judgment.	Has a higher accuracy, since there is no testing fatigue due to the tools and scripts.
Knowledge	Requires just domain knowledge in testing.	Requires both domain knowledge in testing and programming knowledge.

manual. In a semi-automated testing process, the automation might be applied at the beginning of the testing process, in the end, or somewhere in between. Selecting a proper testing procedure aligns with the size of the software product, company policies, and the testing level, which are discussed later in this section. However, each of the mentioned testing procedures has its own advantages, disadvantages, and limitations. Table 2.1 compares the differences between manual and automated testing using different parameters.

2.2.2 Software testing life cycle

As demonstrated in Fig. 2.1, the process of software testing can be divided into several phases, activities, and steps, regardless of the testing procedure (manual, semi-automated, or fully automated). Therefore, it can be described as a cycle known as the software testing life cycle.

In other words, a software testing life cycle is a testing strategy that encompasses a sequence of different activities performed by the testing team to ensure that all features are tested and that all the project's require-

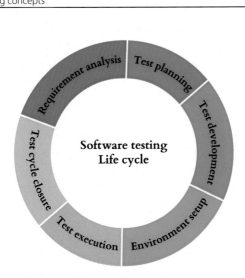

Figure 2.2 A customized version of a software testing life cycle model. Source: Authors' own contribution, inspired by the original model of the software testing life cycle.

ments are met [17]. However, in such as software development life cycle some common activities are usually defined in a software testing life cycle framework, based on the software product size, complexity, and company policies. Fig. 2.2 provides an overview of a typical software testing life cycle, including the following activities:

1. **Requirement analysis.** Requirement analysis refers to the analysis of client and stakeholder system requirements. In this step, the test team analyzes the requirements from a testing perspective. Since this step is the first step of a software development life cycle, some business requirements specification documents need to be shared in advance by the stakeholders. Moreover, the testing team needs to check if all the requirements are testable or not. The decision (e.g., mitigation strategy) about the non-testable requirements and the automation feasibility should be made in this step.

2. **Test planning.** In this step, the required resources (e.g., manpower, tools), cost, and deadline need to be estimated based on the analyzed requirements in the previous step.

3. **Test development.** The required activities in this step are directly related to the testing procedures (manual, semi-automated, or fully automated). Test case specifications and test scripts will be created and generated for the manual and automated testing procedures, respectively. In some testing processes, a requirement traceability matrix needs

to be designed in this step [18]. A typical requirement traceability matrix can guide the testing team to verify whether the requirements are fulfilled via tracking the connections between the requirements, test cases, and test results.

4. **Environment setup.** In this step, the environment information, hardware limitations, and software requirements need to be identified. However, this step can also be performed in an early stage of the testing cycle parallel with the test planning and design.

5. **Test execution.** In this step, all designed test cases need to be executed. Generally, the result of a test case execution can be *Pass*, *Fail*, *Partly Pass*, or *Not Executed*. In some testing cycles, just the *Pass* result is acceptable and all other test results will be reported as *Fail*. Based on the test execution results, several decisions should be made such as bug tracking, troubleshooting, re-execution, or software change request.

6. **Test cycle closure.** Test cycle closure can be considered as the final step where the entire testing cycle should be evaluated based on several criteria, e.g., requirement coverage, time, testing resources, and the achieved quality. Moreover, analyzing each testing cycle might provide some clues to improve the testing cycle (e.g., removing the process bottlenecks) in the future. Usually, a test closure report including a measurement of the mentioned criteria should be prepared and archived.

2.2.3 The levels of software testing

All mentioned activities inside a software testing life cycle can be done at different levels of testing. The following four main levels of testing are applicable to almost all testing processes:

1. **Unit testing.** All individual units (e.g., individual function, components, modules, or objects) of a software product need to be tested. Moreover, the unit tests are usually automated tests, which isolate a section of code and verify its correctness [19].

2. **Integration testing.** Integration testing occurs after unit testing and before system testing, where individual units are combined and tested as a group. In some testing processes, most of the hidden bugs in a software product can only be detected when the units are interacting with each other, which makes the integration testing more complex [20].

3. **System testing.** System testing is performed to validate the complete and fully integrated software product. The entire system needs to be tested as a whole at this level, in order to verify if the system works as expected [21].

4. **Acceptance testing.** A system should be tested for acceptability and delivery. Moreover, the system's compliance with the business requirements needs to be evaluated in this step [22].

Furthermore, *"regression testing"* is another important concept in the software testing domain, which is not a separate level of testing. In fact, regression testing is a type of testing that can be performed during any of the four mentioned software testing levels. The main purpose of performing regression testing is to check if the existing features are affected by code changes [23].

We need to consider that all the four main mentioned testing levels can be fulfilled in different orders. Therefore, several testing models and approaches, such as the *waterfall model, V-model, agile model, spiral model,* and *iterative model,* are proposed in both state of the art and practice. However, selecting a proper testing model is aligned with the project deliverables and the complexity of the project.

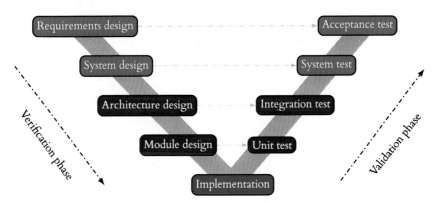

Figure 2.3 The V-model in software testing. Source: Authors' own contribution, inspired by the original V-model.

Fig. 2.3 shows the structure of a typical V-model for testing a software product. As we can see in Fig. 2.3, the *verification* (development) and *validation* (test execution) activities are performed side by side in downhill and uphill shapes. Furthermore, the unit testing is the first level where the acceptance testing must occur as a final level of testing in the V-model. The V-model is a popular approach especially in large industries because it saves time by detecting the defects in an early stage of the testing process. Due to the mentioned advantages, the conducted industrial case studies in this book are mapped with the V-model.

2.3. Test artifacts

Test artifacts are generally referred to as a set of documents (in various formats) that are generated or manually created during the software testing phase in the software development life cycle. Test artifacts should be considered as integral parts of each software testing process that can help the testers track the changes and the recent progress of test activities from the requirements, up to test execution records [24]. Test artifacts can be summarized into the following types: *requirements specification*, *test specification*, *test script*, *software test report*, and *traceability matrix*.

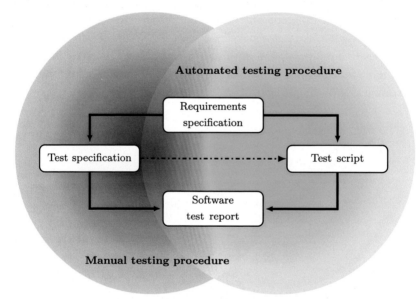

Figure 2.4 A Venn diagram of the software test artifacts. The red zone represents a manual testing process, whereas the green zone indicates an automated (or semi-automated) testing process. Source: Authors' own contribution.

However, the mentioned test artifacts are going to be manually created or automatically generated based on the testing procedure. Fig. 2.4 shows a general overview of the mentioned software test artifacts. As we can see in Fig. 2.4, the red zone represents a manual testing process, whereas the green zone indicates an automated or semi-automated testing process. Moreover, the requirements specification and software test report are held in common in both testing procedures (see the joint part of Fig. 2.4).

Additionally, the presented software test artifacts in Fig. 2.4 also demonstrate a visualized overview of a typical traceability matrix, where the connections between the test artifacts are represented by the arrows. As we can see in Fig. 2.4 the requirements specifications are going to be employed for both creating manual test specifications (see the red zone) and generating the automated test scripts (see the green zone). The dashed arrow in Fig. 2.4 indicates a common way of generating a test script. In some testing processes, the test specifications are going to be utilized for generating the test script. However, there are some tools that just employ the requirements specifications for test script generation. Finally, regardless of the utilized testing procedure, the software test reports need to be created manually (in the text format) or automatically (in a log report format) after each test execution. In order to allow readers to have a better overview of the mentioned test artifacts, some running examples are provided in the upcoming subsections.

2.3.1 Requirements specification

In this subsection, we present a set of requirements specification examples. Requirements specification would normally be performed by a requirements engineer in the team.

Definition 2.4. A requirements specification is a textual document that describes the features and the behavior of a software application [15].

An example of a requirements specification that is extracted from the DOORS database[1] at Alstom Sweden AB[2] is presented in Table 2.2.

As we can see in Table 2.2, information such as requirement ID, name and description, action type, and module number is provided in a requirements specification.

The inserted information in a requirements specification highly depends on the testing domain. For instance, the *Requires* and *Provides* columns in Table 2.2 represent the names of the signals in a train system. Furthermore, through analyzing a requirements specification, in this case, we can derive the signal dependencies between different signals and thereby between the requirements. For instance, signal 273965 is dependent on signal 273957

---

[1] The IBM Rational DOORS Next Generation database is a leading requirements management tool that makes it easy to capture, trace, analyze, and manage changes to information.

[2] Alstom Sweden AB is the largest player in the Swedish railway market, with over 1000 trains delivered. Alstom is a multinational rolling stock manufacturer operating worldwide in rail transport markets, active in the fields of passenger transportation, signaling, and locomotives, with products including the AGV, TGV, Eurostar, Avelia, and New Pendolino high-speed trains, in addition to suburban, regional, and metro trains and Citadis trams.

Table 2.2 A requirements specification example for testing a train system, extracted from the DOORS database at Alstom Sweden AB.

ID	Name	Description	Action type	Link: Requires (>)	Link: Provides (<)	Module
280191	Critical relays status	GIVEN: TCMS receives critical relays status from CTC THEN: TCMS–VDU shall display the critical relays status on car level. Critical relays are shown in ATP-ATO, Propulsion and Brake screens.	Functional	Signal: 273957 Signal: 239030	Signal: 273965	4967

and signal 239030 (see Table 2.2). This concept and also its applications are described later in this book.

2.3.2 Test specification

From the requirements presented in Table 2.2, we can derive several test cases that will cover the requirements. Ensuring that a typical test case covers a requirement is called *requirements coverage*. The requirements coverage is a critical criterion that shows how many requirements have been covered. Moreover, the requirements coverage can also be employed as a factor that can help the testing team to decide to start the test execution or still they need to design more test cases.

Definition 2.5. A test specification is a detailed textual summary of what scenario needs to be tested, how it should be tested, and how often it should be tested, for a given feature of a software product [15].

Natural language tests are often written [25] as a sequence of *Action* and *Reaction* blocks, grouped together and encapsulated in the *Setup* and *Teardown* procedure. In Table 2.3 we provide a test specification example which is designed to test the requirements specification in Table 2.2. As we can see in Table 2.3 it has two separate blocks, one that tests the system under the condition that the train is moving and one that tests it stationary.

As shown in Fig. 2.2, at the test development step the testing team would need to create a test case, test scripts, or any relevant document, based on the testing procedure (manual, semi-automated, or fully automated testing). There are generally some basic criteria, factors, and information that should be followed when creating a test specification based on a requirements specification. A test specification should support the test team to be able to enter and finish the testing phase. As presented in Table 2.3, a test specification should provide the following adequate information:

- **Test case name, ID, tester ID, and date.**
- **Test area (category, test environment).** We need to insert in this block what needs to be verified. Which function group would be tested via executing this test case? This also includes the test execution environment information, e.g., Lab (see the Categories block in Table 2.3).
- **Test level.** Unit, integration, system, or acceptance testing.
- **Test procedure.** Manual, semi-automated, or fully automated.
- **Corresponding requirement.** We need to insert in this block which requirement(s) would be tested. Moreover, this block can help the testing team to measure the requirements coverage factor.

Table 2.3 A test case specification example, designed for testing the presented requirements specification in Table 2.2. The test specification has been extracted from the DOORS database at Alstom Sweden AB.

Test case name: Critic relay	Tester ID:	Date: 2022-03-22	Revision
Test case ID	Test level(s)	Multiple unit operation applicability	
TC-2F-08-01-01-83434	Integration	No	
Categories	Test procedure	Test result	
Function group: 2F Visualisation Execution environment: Lab Single unit operation: Yes	Manual	Passed □, Failed □, Incomplete □ Error □, Not Run □, Inconclusive □	
Requirement(s)	Pre-condition	Post-condition	
280191 Critical relays status	Set train state to TS3.	Set train state to TS1.	
Step	Action	Expected Result	Status
1	Set DT1 cab to Active Set the critical relays status into the ATP-ATO Propulsion and Brake screens.	Verify that the critical relays status on car level is displaying on VDU.	
2	Set no critical relays status in ATP-ATO, Propulsion and Brake screens.	Verify that the critical relays status on car level is not displaying on VDU.	
3	Repeat the above steps for DT2 Cab		

- **Assumptions.** Assumptions include pre-conditions and post-conditions that need to be satisfied before we execute a test case. For instance, before we start the test execution for the presented test specification in Table 2.3, we need to set the *train state to TS3* as a pre-condition. Paying no attention to the test assumption (especially the pre-conditions) might cause an unnecessary failure for a test case. A post-condition is an assumption that indicates the outcome of the test execution.
- **Test scenarios.** This information provides a detailed textual summary of how the test specification can be executed, which should include the following:
  - *Steps to be executed.* This provides an execution order and detailed information of each test step (see Action column in Table 2.3).
  - *Expected result.* This is an ideal test result that the tester should get after each test step is executed (see Table 2.3).
  - *Status.* This represents the actual execution result for each test step. If the actual result differs from the expected results, the difference needs to be reported and documented in the Status block in Table 2.3. More information about the status and test results is described in the forthcoming paragraph.
- **Test result.** This indicates the outcome of each test step, which also concludes the entire test case and thereby the software test life cycle. A test result can be divided into the following groups:
  - *Passed.* A test activity (step in Table 2.3) is deemed to pass if its actual result matches its expected result.
  - *Incomplete.* A test activity does not complete the execution for different reasons.
  - *Failed.* The obtained actual result for a test activity (test step) does not match its expected result.
  - *Error.* This message appears when there is a problem running the test itself (for example, a network error or a mistake in the test script that makes it impossible to continue).
  - *Not run.* This indicates a test activity (test step) that has not yet been run. This execution result is not configurable.
  - *Inconclusive.* This indicates a test activity (test step) that produces a result that is not clear and requires further investigation. We need to consider that the final test result for a test case is an interpretation based on the reported status for each test step, which needs to be made by the testing team and subject matter experts. In some cases, if 80% of test steps are passed the entire test case can be

accepted as passed and it will be removed from the testing cycle. Moreover, the decision regarding the debugging, troubleshooting, merging, adding, or even eliminating a test case will also be made based on the test status results for each test step.

* **Revision.** Based on the obtained test results for each test step and layer for the entire test case, a test case might need to be re-executed, or some changes might be required. Due to the mentioned issues, sometimes, a new revision of a test case is required. This information needs to be inserted in the Revision block in Table 2.3, which shows the history of a test case. Generally, the revision history is highlighted by adding $V1$, $V2$ to the name of a test case.

2.3.3 Test script

As stated earlier in this chapter, a testing process can be performed manually, semi-automatically, or fully automatically. As a test specification is required for manual testing, a test script needs to be generated for testing a software semi-automatically or fully automatically.

Definition 2.6. A test script is a line-by-line instruction that contains the information about the system transactions which need to be tested to validate the system under test [26].

```
pm.test("Response time is less than 200 ms", () => {
  pm.expect(pm.response.responseTime).to.be.below(200);
});
```

Listing 2.1: A test script example for testing response time. The tester can test for the response time to be within a specified range.

A test script can be usually be written in different programming languages such as C# and Java. There are several ways, packages, and libraries that can be employed for generating a test script. The above-presented test script (see the code in Listing 2.1) uses the Postman (pm) library[3] to run the test method.

---

[3] Postman is the way to streamline the process of testing application programming interfaces. Postman Run-time is an open-source library that supports request sending and collection running in the Postman app [27].

2.3.4 Software test report

As explained earlier in this chapter and also presented in Table 2.3, the result of each test execution needs to be reported for all test cases. This documentation process requires a test report which can also be considered as an assessment of how well the test cases are executed.

Definition 2.7. A software test report is a document (in a text format for test specification or test log format for test script) that contains a summary of all test activities (steps) and also the final test results [15].

A test log provides a detailed summary of the overall test execution, including the test results, details, and information about various test steps, the source of issues, and the reasons for failed steps [28]. In Listing 2.2 we provide a customized example of a test log file, for which a description of each row is presented in the upcoming paragraphs.

```
1   <Class="TcSummaryAction">
2   <testName:> Response Time
3   <report>
4     <test-result:> PASS server starts
5     <test-result:> PASS HTTP/1.1 request
6     <test-result> FAIL HTTP/1.0 request
7     <test-result>: PASS server stops
8   <recheck> yes
9   <details>
10    <duration>6523</duration>
11    <errors>0</errors>
12    <timestamp>2021-09-28 09:07:38</timestamp>
13    <warnings>0</warnings>
14  <tcSummaryAction>
```

Listing 2.2: A customized example of a test log file.

- testName. This shows the name of the executed test script. It also might include the project name and the unit name.
- report. This contains the results of the test complete build step. If a test script has several test complete steps, then the results will also have several report nodes.
- test-result. The testing team must utilize this field to register the results of each test case run by a test script. Several test-result fields can be present in the same log file due to support test protocols that allow running more test cases [29]. The recognized test results (e.g.,

PASS, FAIL, Not run, and ERROR) are inserted in the `test-result` field.

- `recheck`. This is a binary Yes or No response. The corresponding test script will not be run if the `recheck` field is present and defined as No. It might be the case that two or more `recheck` fields appear in the same log file, which can be considered as undefined behavior [29].
- `details`. This provides more detailed information for the execution, such as:
  - `duration`. This shows the test run duration in milliseconds. Generally, the test run duration is rounded down to seconds. For example, for a test running for 6.122 seconds, this node will return 6000.
  - `errors`. This indicates the number of errors that are encountered during the test execution. As we can see in the provided example in Listing 2.2, `errors` is equal to 0.
  - `timestamp`. This indicates a year (`2021`), month (`September`), day (`28`), and time (`09:07:38`) am. Two timestamps are usually separated by a hyphen (`-`). The timestamp shows each record in the test log file.
  - `warnings`. This shows the number of warnings encountered to the log during the test execution.

2.3.4.1 Test summary

A test summary is another software test report that officially summarizes the test results of all executed test cases, including the total number of executed test cases and the pass and fail percentages.

Fig. 2.5 illustrates a part of a test summary report. As we can see, some test cases are completely passed or failed (see TC59 and TC60). However, having more than one result (e.g., TC58) for a test case indicates the test execution results for different steps of a test case. For instance, 4 steps of a test case passed while the remaining steps failed. The test summary report can usually be shared with the stakeholders, and it can also be employed for test execution analysis, as shown in Fig. 2.6.

2.3.5 Traceability matrix

In an agile testing process, all the mentioned artifacts, documents, and reports should be connected together, where the testing team, test managers, and stakeholders can track the progress of a testing process. There are different solutions and models for tracing the testing process, all the way through definition, design, development, and testing, where some of the models are

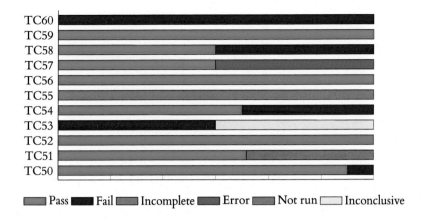

Figure 2.5 An example of a test summary report. Source: Authors' own contribution.

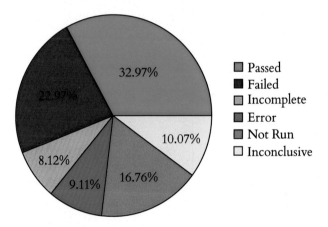

Figure 2.6 Test execution analysis using the test summary report. Source: Authors' own contribution.

implemented as a tool or database, e.g., the DOORS database. The mentioned concept can be introduced as a traceability matrix which is a critical test artifact. Generally, a traceability matrix aims to verify if all requirements are tested and no functionality is unchecked during the testing process.

Definition 2.8. A traceability matrix is usually a tabulated document that correlates and traces the initial list of requirements to their implementation (test case specification, test script) and test results [15].

Table 2.4 shows an example of the resulting view of a traceability matrix extracted from the DOORS database at Alstom Sweden AB. In the pre-

Table 2.4 An example of the resulting view of a traceability matrix extracted from the DOORS database at Alstom Sweden AB. Source: DOORS database.

BTI/FVDS ID	SRS	SRS PUID	OSTS	OSTS PUID	OSTS lab test results
4S–09–05–04–C30	TCMS (BL 13.0)	SR–C30–SRS–REQ–813 ⇑	OSTS function and frame-work	IVV–C30–SyTR–functionfram–IVV–021 ⇑	Passed
4S–09–06–08–C30	TCMS (BL 13.0)	SR–C30–SRS–REQ–2074 ⇑	OSTS communication	IVV–C30–SyTR–communication–IVV–023 ⇑	Passed

sented example, BTI/FVDS indicates the Source input requirement, SRS and SRS PUID show the software requirement ID, OSTS is the test specification, and OSTS PUID shows the test case ID. Moreover, the OSTS lab test results in Table 2.4 show the results as reported in the test record (OSTR). By clicking on the arrows ($\Longrightarrow$) in Table 2.4 we can trace the created test cases for each requirement and also monitor the test results.

2.4. The evolution of software testing

The history of software testing began with debugging terminology mentioned by Grace Murray Hopper[4] for defining minor computer problems in 1947 [30]. However, due to the lack of proper functioning of the existing software in the 1940s, the testing process was more focused on the hardware components.

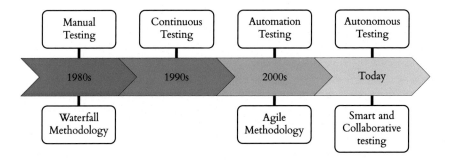

Figure 2.7 A summary of the evolution of software testing. Source: Authors' own contribution.

The initial efforts of software adoption for the pre-designed requirements were started in the 1950s by Alan Turing[5] and software was later developed by Charles Baker[6]. *The Turing Test* can be considered as one of

---

[4] Grace Brewster Murray Hopper (1906–1992) was an American computer scientist. She is best known for her trailblazing contributions to the development of computer languages [30].

[5] Alan Mathison Turing (1912–1954) was a British mathematician and logician who made major contributions to mathematics, cryptanalysis, logic, mathematical biology, computer science, and artificial intelligence [31].

[6] Charles L. Baker has directed and participated in systems analysis, design, and computer programming projects in the application areas of aircraft and aerospace engineering, military command and control, and also modeling and forecasting and business data processing [32].

the first articles which were written in the software testing and artificial intelligence domain [33].

Until the late 1970s, testing was strongly linked to debugging, where Glenford Myers[7] for the first time proposed the separation theory of debugging from testing [34]. While software products and their quality assurance had received a great deal of attention in the 1970–1980s, proper methodology for testing appeared to be lacking.

In Fig. 2.7 we illustrate a summary of the software testing development process. Although some of the highlighted methodologies in Fig. 2.7 have waned over recently, the newer versions of them still remain a common design process in the industry.

As we can see in Fig. 2.7, the waterfall model was employed as a new method for the software development process in the early 1980s. However, the waterfall methodology was first proposed by Winston Royce[8] in 1970 (see [35]). The key feature of the waterfall model was its logical progression of cascading down steps including requirement analysis, design, implementation, testing, operation, and maintenance. The waterfall model has a continuous process, where later, other researchers proposed other simultaneous processes such as the V-model (see Fig. 2.3) using the initial idea of the logical progression of the waterfall model. One of the biggest game-changers in the testing world and quality assurance was the concept of continuous testing which involves testing at every stage of the software development life cycle [36]. The appearance of continuous testing has two main advantages: (1) for the first time software testing was accepted as a separate process of the software development life cycle and (2) it was the first attempt of evaluating the quality of the software as part of a continuous delivery process.

At that time most of the attempts for performing testing were manual. Although manual testing had its own advantages, it could not meet the huge testing volumes, quality, and market demands in a very limited time. In fact, the rapid diffusion of information technology in the 1990s had a direct consequence on the existing testing methodologies. Therefore, the demand for new, agile, and automated methods for testing was highlighted

---

[7] Glenford J. Myers is an American computer scientist, entrepreneur, and author. He authored several textbooks in the computer sciences such as *The Art of Software Testing*, *Software Reliability: Principles and Practices*, and *Composite/Structured Design*. Myers has made important contributions to microprocessor architecture [34].

[8] Winston Walker Royce (1929–1995) was an American computer scientist. He was best known for his research for the waterfall model for the software development life cycle [35].

Table 2.5 A summary of some conducted research for employing artificial intelligence techniques in the software testing field.

Author	Application in software testing	Method
Adamo et al. [37]	Automating test design and execution of graphical user interface testing of Android apps	Reinforcement Learning
Almagharbe et al. [38]	Classifying of the test results	Semi-supervised Learning
Cao et al. [39]	Anomaly detection in web log files	Supervised learning
Chetouane et al. [40]	Test suite minimization	Unsupervised learning
Dharmalingam et al. [41]	Optimal test sequences and test case generation	Intelligent agents
Frounchi et al. [42]	Oracle construction for automatic test evaluation	Machine learning
Hall et al. [43]	Predicting software fault	Supervised learning
Hemmati et al. [44]	Predicting test case failure for manual testing	Natural language processing
Kalibhat et al. [45]	Troubleshooting of the software products	Machine learning
Pham et al. [46]	Predicting task execution time	Supervised learning
Memon et al. [47]	Planning the automated test design	Artificial intelligence
Ramler et al. [48]	Detection and prediction based on classifiers for risk-based testing	Machine learning
Roy et al. [49]	Forecasting of software reliability	Neural network
Roychowdhury et al. [50]	Localization of software faults	Feature selection
Sekhon et al. [51]	Improving and generalizing end-to-end testing methods	Deep learning
Seliya et al. [52]	Estimating software quality	Semi-supervised learning
Silva et al. [53]	Estimating required execution efforts of software testing	Machine learning
Singh [54]	Evaluating requirements specifications	Machine learning
Tahvili et al. [55]	Stochastic scheduling of manual integration test cases	Natural language processing
Verma et al. [56]	Test case generation using software requirements specification	Natural language processing

increasingly. However, reviewing the history of software testing shows that some approaches for test automation and automatic test generation have been developed by different companies such as Mercury Interactive and IBM before the 1990s. But test automation has been taken most seriously some years later, yielding results such as the provided solutions for the test automation design techniques by Fewster and Graham [57] and Buwalda et al. [58]. Another topic that has received a great deal of attention was agile testing. The term agile in the context of software development represents the adaptive capacity and response to change [59]. Utilizing the agile approach in software development was a proper solution to identify and thereby deal with an uncertain and turbulent environment. In this regard, agile testing indicates a continuous but non-sequential testing practice that needs to follow the rules and principles of agile software development. The presented customized version of a software testing life cycle in Fig. 2.2 is an example of an agile testing approach that includes test planning, infrastructure, test environments, etc.

Receiving swift feedback and adaptiveness can be considered a big movement in software development. However, the rapid rate of technological and digital changes required even more agile approaches. Thus the need for automated creation and analysis of tests was increasingly highlighted. On the other hand, artificial intelligence has started to grow into a formidable tool in the middle of the 2000s, where the computer could think and also act as a human brain. Matching the demands and the existing artificial intelligence algorithms is leading to the creation of autonomous tests, reducing the human intervention and, more importantly, the workload. However, we need to consider that the capabilities of autonomous testing using artificial intelligence models are still relatively new. Therefore we need to differentiate fact from fiction. First, most of the current solutions are not applicable in all areas. Second, most of the applicable solutions are not fully autonomous yet, where they can be assistive in the software development life cycle [60].

And, as a final word in this chapter, some of the conducted researches in the area of software testing and artificial intelligence are presented in Table 2.5. As we can see in Table 2.5 the proposed AI-based approaches are highlighted where each of them has different applications in the software testing domain.

References

[1] P. Ammann, J. Offutt, Introduction to Software Testing, Cambridge University Press, 2008.

[2] N. Ruparelia, Software development lifecycle models, SIGSOFT Software Engineering Notes 35 (3) (2010) 8–13.

[3] C. Ebert, G. Gallardo, J. Hernantes, N. Serrano, DevOps, IEEE Software 33 (3) (2016) 94–100.

[4] L. Zhu, L. Bass, G. Champlin-Scharff, DevOps and its practices, IEEE Software 33 (3) (2016) 32–34.

[5] S. Robertson, J. Robertson, Mastering the Requirements Process, ACM Press Books, Addison-Wesley, 2006.

[6] R. Fulton, R. Vandermolen, Airborne Electronic Hardware Design Assurance: A Practitioner's Guide to RTCA/DO-254, CRC Press, 2017.

[7] K. Sahu, R. Pandey, R. Kumar, Risk management perspective in SDLC, International Journal of Computer Science and Software Engineering 4 (2014) 1247–1251.

[8] A. Pranam, The End-to-End Product Journey, Apress, 2018, pp. 13–17.

[9] A. Aleti, B. Buhnova, L. Grunske, A. Koziolek, I. Meedeniya, Software architecture optimization methods: A systematic literature review, IEEE Transactions on Software Engineering 39 (5) (2013) 658–683.

[10] G. Piccoli, Information Systems for Managers: Texts and Cases, Wiley, 2008.

[11] M. Sharma, A study of SDLC to develop well engineered software, International Journal of Advanced Research in Computer Science 8 (3) (2017) 520–523.

[12] P. Davachelvan, Evolving a new model (SDLC Model-2010) for software development life cycle (SDLC), 2010.

[13] S. Radack, The system development life cycle (SDLC), 2009.

[14] E. Alegroth, R. Feldt, P. Kolstrom, Maintenance of automated test suites in industry: An empirical study on visual GUI testing, Information and Software Technology 73 (February 2016).

[15] IEEE Guide for Developing System Requirements Specifications, IEEE Standard 1233-1996, 1996, pp. 1–30.

[16] ISO/IEC/IEEE International Standard – Systems and Software Engineering – Vocabulary, ISO/IEC/IEEE 24765:2017(E), 2017, pp. 1–541.

[17] N. Honest, Role of testing in software development life cycle, International Journal of Computer Sciences and Engineering 7 (2019) 886–889.

[18] G. Duraisamy, R. Atan, Requirement traceability matrix through documentation for scrum methodology, Journal of Theoretical and Applied Information Technology 52 (2013) 154–159.

[19] R. Osherove, The Art of Unit Testing: With Examples in NET, Manning Pubs Co Series, Manning, 2009.

[20] S. Tahvili, Multi-criteria optimization of system integration testing, PhD thesis, Malardalen University, December 2018.

[21] T. Wu, Y. Dong, Y. Zhang, A. Singa, Extendaist: Exploring the space of AI-in-the-loop system testing, Applied Sciences 10 (2) (2020).

[22] B. Hambling, P. Van Goethem, User Acceptance Testing: A Step-by-step Guide, BCS, 2013.

[23] A. Maspupah, A. Rahmani, J. Min, Comparative study of regression testing tools feature on unit testing, Journal of Physics: Conference Series 1869 (1) (2021) 012098.

[24] R. Parizi, S. Lee, M. Dabbagh, Achievements and challenges in state-of-the-art software traceability between test and code artifacts, IEEE Transactions on Reliability 63 (4) (2014) 913–926.

[25] A. da Silva, A. Paiva, V. da Silva, A test specification language for information systems based on data entities, use cases and state machines, in: S. Hammoudi, L.F. Pires, B. Selic (Eds.), Model-Driven Engineering and Software Development, Springer International Publishing, Cham, 2019, pp. 455–474.

[26] C. Leandro, C. Ricardo, d.O. Flavio, R. Elder, d.S. Maicon, Z. Avelino, Generating performance test scripts and scenarios based on abstract intermediate models, in: Proceedings of the 24th International Conference on Software Engineering & Knowledge Engineering (SEKE'2012), Knowledge Systems Institute Graduate School, 2012, pp. 112–117.

[27] S. Rahalkar, Testing Mobile Apps and APIs with Burp Suite, Apress, 2021, pp. 147–164.

[28] A. Chuvakin, K. Schmidt, C. Phillips, Logging and Log Management: The Authoritative Guide to Understanding the Concepts Surrounding Logging and Log Management, Elsevier Science, 2012.

[29] G. Vaughan, GNU Autoconf, Automake, and Libtool, New Riders, 2000.

[30] K. Beyer, Grace Hopper and the Invention of the Information Age, Lemelson Center Studies in Invention and Innovation Series, MIT Press, 2012.

[31] J. Bowen, Z. Liu, Z. Zhang, Engineering Trustworthy Software Systems: Second International School, SETSS 2016, Chongqing, China, March 28 – April 2, 2016, Tutorial Lectures, Lecture Notes in Computer Science, Springer International Publishing, 2017.

[32] T. Cheatham, Biography of Charles L. Baker, Association for Computing Machinery, 1978, pp. 512–513.

[33] A. Saygin, I. Cicekli, V. Akman, Turing test: 50 years later, Minds and Machines 10 (1999) 2000.

[34] G. Myers, C. Sandler, T. Badgett, T. Thomas, The Art of Software Testing, Business Data Processing: A Wiley Series, Wiley, 2004.

[35] W. Royce, Managing the development of large software systems: Concepts and techniques, in: Proceedings of the 9th International Conference on Software Engineering, ICSE '87, IEEE Computer Society Press, 1987, pp. 328–338.

[36] B. Rady, R. Coffin, Continuous Testing with Ruby, Rails, and JavaScript, Pragmatic Bookshelf Series, Pragmatic Bookshelf, 2011.

[37] D. Adamo, K. Khan, S. Koppula, R. Bryce, Reinforcement learning for Android GUI testing, in: Proceedings of the 9th ACM SIGSOFT International Workshop on Automating TEST Case Design, Selection, and Evaluation, 2018, pp. 2–8.

[38] R. Almaghairbe, M. Roper, Automatically classifying test results by semi-supervised learning, in: 2016 IEEE 27th International Symposium on Software Reliability Engineering (ISSRE), 2016, pp. 116–126.

[39] Q. Cao, Y. Qiao, Z. Lyu, Machine learning to detect anomalies in web log analysis, in: 2017 3rd IEEE International Conference on Computer and Communications (ICCC), 2017, pp. 519–523.

[40] N. Chetouane, F. Wotawa, H. Felbinger, M. Nica, On using k-means clustering for test suite reduction, in: 2020 IEEE International Conference on Software Testing, Verification and Validation Workshops (ICSTW), 2020, pp. 380–385.

[41] J. Dharmalingam, V. Mohan, Intelligentester – test sequence optimization framework using multi-agents, Journal of Computers 3 (June 2008).

[42] K. Frounchi, L. Briand, L. Grady, Y. Labiche, R. Subramanyan, Automating image segmentation verification and validation by learning test oracles, Information and Software Technology 53 (12) (2011) 1337–1348.

[43] T. Hall, D. Bowes, The state of machine learning methodology in software fault prediction, in: 11th International Conference on Machine Learning and Applications, vol. 2, 2012, pp. 308–313.

[44] H. Hemmati, F. Sharifi, Investigating NLP-based approaches for predicting manual test case failure, in: 2018 IEEE 11th International Conference on Software Testing, Verification and Validation (ICST), 2018, pp. 309–319.

[45] N. Kalibhat, S. Varshini, C. Kollengode, D. Sitaram, S. Kalambur, Software troubleshooting using machine learning, in: 2017 IEEE 24th International Conference on High Performance Computing Workshops (HiPCW), 2017, pp. 3–10.

[46] T. Pham, J. Durillo, T. Fahringer, Predicting workflow task execution time in the cloud using a two-stage machine learning approach, IEEE Transactions on Cloud Computing 8 (1) (2020) 256–268.

[47] A. Memon, M. Pollack, M. Soffa, A planning-based approach to GUI testing, in: Proceedings of the 13th International Software/Internet Quality Week, 2000.

[48] R. Ramler, M. Felderer, Requirements for integrating defect prediction and risk-based testing, in: 2016 42th Euromicro Conference on Software Engineering and Advanced Applications (SEAA), IEEE, 2016, pp. 359–362.

[49] P. Roy, G. Mahapatra, K. Dey, Forecasting of software reliability using neighborhood fuzzy particle swarm optimization based novel neural network, IEEE/CAA Journal of Automatica Sinica 6 (6) (2019) 1365–1383.

[50] S. Roychowdhury, S. Khurshid, Software fault localization using feature selection, in: Proceedings of the International Workshop on Machine Learning Technologies in Software Engineering, MALETS '11, Association for Computing Machinery, New York, NY, USA, 2011, pp. 11–18.

[51] J. Sekhon, C. Fleming, Towards improved testing for deep learning, in: 2019 IEEE/ACM 41st International Conference on Software Engineering: New Ideas and Emerging Results (ICSE-NIER), 2019, pp. 85–88.

[52] N. Seliya, T. Khoshgoftaar, Software quality estimation with limited fault data: a semi-supervised learning perspective, Software Quality Journal 15 (2007) 327–344.

[53] D. Silva, M. Jino, B. Abreu, Machine learning methods and asymmetric cost function to estimate execution effort of software testing, in: Third International Conference on Software Testing, Verification and Validation, 2010, pp. 275–284.

[54] M. Singh, Automated validation of requirement reviews: A machine learning approach, in: 2018 IEEE 26th International Requirements Engineering Conference (RE), 2018, pp. 460–465.

[55] S. Tahvili, R. Pimentel, W. Afzal, M. Ahlberg, E. Fornander, M. Bohlin, sortes: A supportive tool for stochastic scheduling of manual integration test cases, Journal of IEEE Access 6 (2019) 1–19.

[56] R. Verma, R. Beg, Generation of test cases from software requirements using natural language processing, in: 2013 6th International Conference on Emerging Trends in Engineering and Technology, 2013, pp. 140–147.

[57] M. Fewster, D. Graham, Software Test Automation: Effective Use of Test Execution Tools, ACM Press Series, Addison-Wesley, 1999.

[58] H. Buwalda, D. Janssen, I. Pinkster, P. Watters, Integrated Test Design and Automation: Using the Test Frame Method, Addison-Wesley, 2002.

[59] K. Beck, M. Beedle, A. Bennekum, A. Cockburn, W. Cunningham, M. Fowler, J. Grenning, J. Highsmith, A. Hunt, R. Jeffries, J. Kern, B. Marick, R. Martin, S. Mellor, K. Schwaber, J. Sutherland, D. Thomas, Manifesto for agile software development, 2013.

[60] F. Ricca, A. Marchetto, A. Stocco, AI-based test automation: A grey literature analysis, 2021, pp. 263–270.

CHAPTER THREE

Transformation, vectorization, and optimization

Chapter points

- This chapter provides an introduction to and review of the history of text analytics.
- Several industrial examples of text analytics applications are presented.
- A comprehensive introduction to the concepts of vectorization, transformation, machine learning, neural networks, deep learning, and natural language processing is given.
- A brief introduction to imbalanced learning, applications, and solutions is presented.
- Some machine learning-based solution examples for dimensionality reduction and visualization are provided.

"We can build a much brighter future where humans are relieved of menial work using AI capabilities."

Andrew Ng

As we demonstrated in Chapter 2, most of the test artifacts have a textual format regardless of whether they are created manually (e.g., the requirement and test specifications in Table 2.2 and Table 2.3, respectively) or they are machine-generated (such as log files presented in Listing 2.2). Having a large set of text documents in various formats and levels of organization (unstructured and structured) pushes us to apply novel text analytics methods in the testing domain. However, it is not the first time that text analytics are heavily involved with a variety of different technologies. In the upcoming section, we review the history and roots of text analytics and analyze how it has become a game-changer in the area of software engineering and especially in the software testing domain.

3.1. A review of the history of text analytics

Text analytics is the process of converting large volumes of unstructured text into structured quantitative data to provide a search facility for exploring insights, trends, and patterns [1]. Text analysis (which is roughly

*Artificial Intelligence Methods for Optimization of
the Software Testing Process*
https://doi.org/10.1016/B978-0-32-391913-5.00014-2

synonymous with text mining) involves several aspects and sub-disciplines such as lexical analysis, pattern recognition, parsing, part-of-speech tagging, etc.

Although text analytics has a long history in the social sciences [2], in the past decade it has been transformed by new technologies. During the Second World War, a call for action to increase investment in research and technological development of text analytics was launched. The purpose of the grant decision was to support investments in the potential research opportunities of *"content analysis"* by the governments [3].

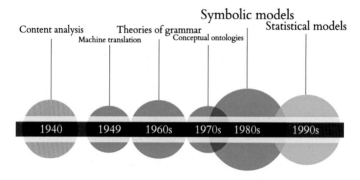

Figure 3.1 The stages of the text analytics practice from World War II until the 1990s. Source: Authors' own contribution.

Text analytics became a new technology during the Second World War for translating the words and phrases captured from unstructured data into numerical representations. However, text analytics emerged as an independent discipline in the early 1960s, although content analysis was invented some two decades earlier. On the other hand, the conducted research on text analytics has not followed a straightforward plan [3]. During the 45 years after the end of the Second World War, researchers started to use text as data, which gave rise to an applied version of text analytics. Fig. 3.1 shows a brief overview of the history of the text analytics from the Second World War until the 1990s.

In 1949, Warren Weaver[1] proposed the possibility of employing digital computers for translating the natural language, which was a turning point in the field of machine translation [6]. In contrast to today's machine translation, the old machine translation employed a bounded dictionary including

---

[1] Warren Weaver (July 17, 1894–November 24, 1978) was an American scientist, mathematician, and science administrator [5]. Weaver is recognized as one of the pioneers of machine translation and as an important figure in creating support for science in the USA.

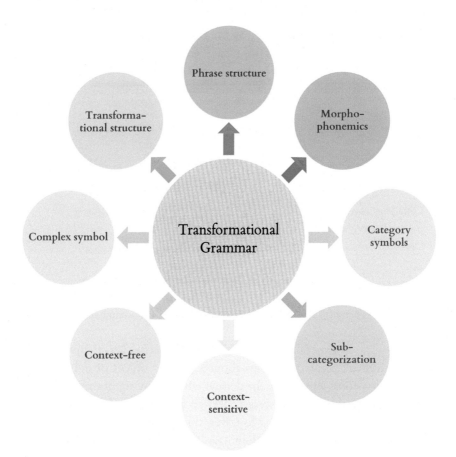

Figure 3.2 The key concepts and rules of transformational grammar (also called transformational-generative grammar [TGG]). Source: Authors' own contribution inspired by Adetuyi and Fidelis [4].

some appropriate words for translation. Considering the limits of generalizability, inefficiency, ambiguity, and the results, the initial idea for a rule-based system of syntactic structures [7] was generated in 1957. Within a few years, some new theories of grammar were born which ended up formulating the transformational-generative grammar (TGG). TGG simply employs the illustrated key concepts and rules in Fig. 3.2 to generate new sentences, where all the mentioned key concepts and rules have the same level of importance.

The building of a conceptual ontology in the early 1970s can be considered as a first attempt to transfer real-world information into computer-understandable data [8]. However, inefficiency and poor achieved results by conceptual ontologies indicated that the research needed to be continued in the text analytics domain. In this regard, in the 1980s a new terminology for solving the text analytics problem was born, which is called *symbolic modeling*, which refers to human-readable and explainable processes.

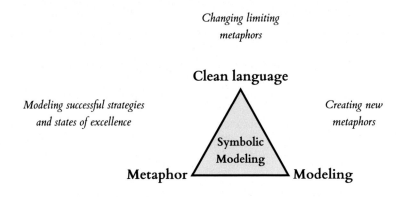

Figure 3.3 The structure of symbolic modeling. Source: Authors' own contribution.

Symbolism, in general, refers to different approaches for creating logical rules and informative relationships about a specific object or concept [9]. The 1980s are considered to be the decade when many significant problems in the text analytics domain were addressed by applying several symbolic approaches (see [10] and [11]). Moreover, this attempt was the first step of complex hard-coded rules and grammars to parse language; therefore, the symbolic methods are known as *good old-fashioned artificial intelligence* [12]. Fig. 3.3 shows a schematic overview of the architecture of symbolic modeling.

As we can see in Fig. 3.3 a text is divided into some tokens (e.g., words and punctuation). Later, some meanings need to be manually assigned to those tokens, which makes them easier to debug, explain, and control. Besides the mentioned advantages of symbolic modeling, in closely related applications, knowledge transfer is also possible [12]. With the dramatically accelerating pace of the development and adoption of new technologies in the 1980*s*, the symbolic models could not adapt to the changes. As the main disadvantages of them, we can mention the lack of interpretability and the required time and computation power for analyzing large amounts of data [13]. Considering the mentioned issues and the increase of computational power in the 1990s, the statistical models have emerged to break the old and complex sets of hand-written rules for text analysis [14]. Moreover, the main advantage of employing the statistical models is their ability to make probabilistic decisions [15].

However, since technology is inevitable in our everyday lives, having more efficient and accurate technology is always desirable. The process of analyzing the enormous amounts of text data in order to extract information has become the major role of text analytics since the 2000s.

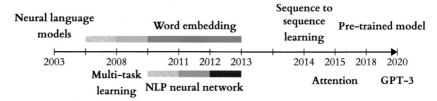

Figure 3.4 The stages of text analytics in the artificial intelligence era. Source: Authors' own contribution, inspired by Krippendorff [3].

In Fig. 3.4 we present a perspective on the text analytics development process in the 21st century. It is obvious from Fig. 3.4 that artificial intelligence had a high impact on the text analytics area, where it is heavily involved with the different sub-disciplines of artificial intelligence such as machine learning, neural networks, and natural language processing. The main driver for artificial intelligence applications in text analytics is the high demand for unsupervised and semi-supervised learning algorithms. Moreover, a rapid increase in the text data within the growth of the websites has resulted in the demand for fast computational techniques for analyzing natural text [16]. Since most of the employed methods in the upcoming chapters are related to machine learning, neural networks, and deep learning, in the following sections we are mainly focusing on the impact of the mentioned topics on text analytics.

3.1.1 Text analytics sub-disciplines and applications

Fig. 3.5 demonstrates an overview of text analytics and its aspects from the beginning, which draws upon various techniques and applications in a broader field of text analytics.

Miner et al. [1] have categorized text analytics into seven sub-disciplines. In this book we are trying to map the proposed sub-disciplines to the faced challenges and use cases in the industry (see Fig. 3.5). The following paragraphs provide a brief description of the presented sub-disciplines in Fig. 3.5 by Miner et al. [1].

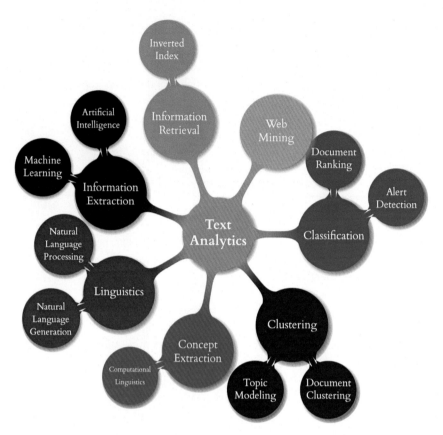

Figure 3.5 An overview of the sub-disciplines and aspects of text analytics and how they relate. Source: Authors' own contribution, inspired by Miner et al. [1].

- **Information retrieval.** Discovering knowledge by the automated analysis of free text is a field of research that is evolving from information retrieval and is often called text mining [17], [18]. As an example of information retrieval, we have an inverted index that is a database index storing a mapping from content, such as words or numbers, to its locations in a table or in a document or a set of documents (see Fig. 3.6).
- **Web mining.** Web mining is the process of converting raw data to useful information using the content of a web pages [19]. The process starts with the extraction of structured data or information from web pages and then integrates with related data. As the web pages are directly linked using hyperlinks, this exposes a layer of the connectedness

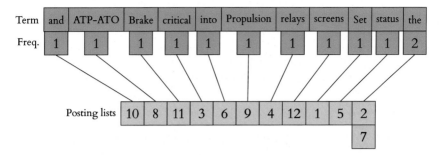

Figure 3.6 An example of the inverted index structure using the segment "Set the critical relays status into the ATP-ATO Propulsion and Brake screens" from the presented test case in Table 2.3. Source: Authors' own contribution.

of the data that is gathered by web mining. Depending on the structure of the test cases and requirements, many of the web mining approaches (Fig. 3.7) can be used. For example, signal connections between test cases can be observed as links or they can be linked through the shared requirements.

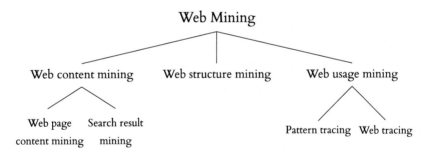

Figure 3.7 Sub-disciplines of web mining. Source: Authors' own contribution, inspired by Shah and Pandit [19].

- **Text classification.** Text classification is the process of classifying documents into pre-defined categories based on their content.
  Text classification is the primary requirement of text retrieval systems, which retrieve a text in response to a user query. Employing text classification can help us to transform a text in any form of producing summaries, answering questions, or extracting data. Text classification has a broad range of applications in everyday life such as spam detection (see Fig. 3.8) and intent detection. Most of the existing supervised learning algorithms need a sufficient number of text documents to automatically learn and accurately classify a text. However, instead of

Incoming emails

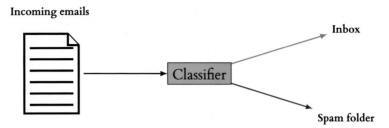

Figure 3.8 An example of text classification. The model is used to flag incoming emails as spam. Source: Authors' own contribution.

using large text documents, the relation between the words such as association rules can be used to derive feature sets from pre-classified text documents. The naive Bayes classifier is highly recommended to be applied on derived features. Finally, only a single concept of genetic algorithm can be added for the classification [20].

- **Document clustering.** Document clustering is the task of grouping a set of unlabeled texts in such a way that texts in the same cluster are more similar to each other than to those in other clusters. Text cluster-ing algorithms process text and determine if natural clusters (groups) exist in the data [21]. Document clustering can be commonly used for text filtering, topic extraction, fast information retrieval, and also document organization [22].
  Broadly, clustering can be divided into two groups (see Fig. 3.9):
  - **Hard clustering.** Hard clustering groups items such that each item is assigned to only one cluster. For example, we want to know if a tweet is expressing a positive or negative sentiment. k–Means is a hard clustering algorithm.
  - **Soft clustering.** Sometimes we do not need a binary answer; soft clustering is grouping items such that an item can belong to multiple clusters. Fuzzy C-means is a soft clustering algorithm.
- **Topic modeling.** Topic modeling represents the statistical model-ing techniques that can discover patterns of words in a collection of text documents [23]. Latent semantic analysis (LSA), probabilistic LSA (pLSA), and latent Dirichlet allocation are three examples of the most common techniques for topic modeling. Topic modeling generally can be employed to cluster documents by giving a probability distribution over a range of topics for each document. Topic modeling can be con-sidered as a soft clustering (see clusters C_2 and C_3 in Fig. 3.9), where

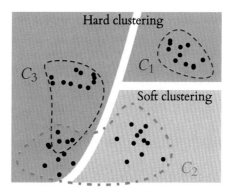

Figure 3.9 An example of hard and soft text clustering, where C_1 is an example of hard clustering and C_2 and C_3 are two examples of soft clustering. Source: Authors' own contribution.

each data point has a probabilistic degree of ownership to each cluster [23].

- **Concept extraction.** Concept extraction focuses on extracting concepts of interest from one or more text documents. It has been adapted to computationally extract clinical information from text for a wide range of applications ranging from clinical decision support to care quality improvement [24].

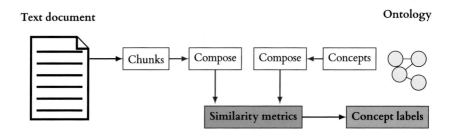

Figure 3.10 Process of concept extraction. Source: Authors' own contribution, inspired by Tulkens et al. [25].

Fig. 3.10 shows a structure of such a system. It creates representations of concepts from the restricted medical language by combining natural language descriptions of concepts with word representations and composing these into higher-order concept vectors. The resulting concept vectors are then used to assign labels to candidate phrases.

- **Natural language processing.** natural language processing is a branch of linguistic studies and artificial intelligence that helps computers understand, interpret, and manipulate human languages. Natural language processing is broadly defined as the automatic manipulation of natural language such as speech and text by software [26].

- **Natural language generation.** Natural language generation is one of the main branches of linguistic studies. Report production and image captions are the most common uses of natural language generation. In fact, natural language generation commonly uses a multi-stage process, with each step further refining the data being used to produce content with natural-sounding language. Several different approaches are proposed for natural language generation [27–31], where most of the proposed solutions are focusing on the six stages of natural language generation. In this book, we review and summarize some of the proposed frameworks for natural text generation, as a pipeline shown in Fig. 3.11.

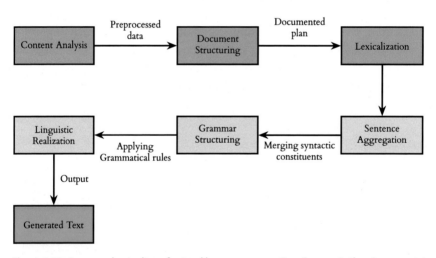

Figure 3.11 An example pipeline of natural language generation. Source: Authors' own contribution, inspired by the proposed frameworks by Reiter and Dale [32] and Banaee et al. [30].

Definition 3.1. A corpus is a language resource consisting of a large and structured set of texts [33].

1. Content analysis and pattern identification. This step focuses on data filtering, where we should decide which part of the data needs to be in the content produced and which data needs to be eliminated at the end of this process. In this step, some possible errors and distortions which might exist in the stored data should be removed

from the dataset. Tokenization, normalization, and noise removal are the main activities that need to be done. The main topics in the source document and their relationships should be identified in this step. We will also deal with data interpretation, data integration, and pattern recognition, which aims to provide a unified and consistent view of the dataset. Employing machine learning algorithms such as classification, clustering methods, and ensemble learning algorithms is often suggested at this stage [34].

2. Document structuring. After applying the proposed approaches in step 1, we have pre-processed integrated text data that can be utilized for creating a documented plan. In fact, in this step, we need to design the order of sentences in a generated text [35]. Schemas [36], corpus-based approaches [37], and heuristic approaches [38] can be mentioned as the most popular methods for document structuring in this step.

3. Lexicalization. In this step, we need to select the content words such as nouns, verbs, adjectives, and adverbs for the generated text [32]. Lexicalization also allows us to be sensitive to a specific word. Wang et al. [39] proposed a Python-based interface for wide-coverage lexicalized tree-adjoining grammars.

4. Sentence aggregation. In order to correctly summarize a topic, we need to merge syntactic constituents in this step. In other words, the most relevant sentences or parts of each sentence need to be combined. In this step, we need to decide when and how two constituents need to be aggregated via designing an aggregated structure. Gatt and Reiter [40] proposed a Java library called SimpleNLG[2] as a realization engine for English that provides both simple and robust interfaces to generate syntactic structures.

5. Grammatical structuring. It might be the case that the text data does not have a correct grammatical structure. In this step, by applying several grammatical rules we can generate a grammatically structured text. As other presented steps in Fig. 3.11 there are several grammar development platforms to perform grammatical structuring such as MedSLT Regulus [41], which was originally developed to translate doctor–patient examination dialogs [42].

---

[2] SimpleNLG defines a set of lexical and phrasal types, corresponding to the major grammatical categories, as well as ways of combining these and setting various feature values [40].

Most of the existing programs deduce the syntactical structure of the sentence. This information can be employed later to rewrite the sentence in a grammatically correct manner [42].

6. Linguistic realization and language presentation. Employing linguistic realization can help us produce a text which is syntactically, morphologically, and also orthographically correct [32]. In fact, in the final step, the output will be generated based on a template or format that the end-user or programmer has selected.

Content creation and chatterbots are the most important applications of natural language generation in the artificial intelligence era. However, employing the proposed pipeline in Fig. 3.11 has several applications in the software testing domain. For instance, by analyzing the requirements specifications, we are able to generate the test specifications automatically [43,44].

- **Information extraction.** Information extraction distills structured data or knowledge from an unstructured text by identifying references to named entities as well as stated relationships between such entities [45]. As mentioned before, one of the main goals of data analytics and data-mining is to derive relevant information from a natural text. In this regard, information extraction can be considered as an important approach to text mining involving the use of natural language information extraction which is able to locate specific items in a natural text document. Information extraction has several applications; it can simply be employed for relationship identification, pattern matching, and extracting structured information from unstructured text [46]. Therefore, the use of classifiers, sequence modeling approaches [47], and hand-written regular expressions [48] is generally recommended for information extraction tasks.
  Mooney and Nahm [46] proposed DISCOVERY FROM TEXT EXTRACTION (DISCOTEX) as a framework for text mining. DISCOTEX is an example to show how a learned information extraction system can transform a natural language document into more structured data. Moreover, Robust Automated Production of Information Extraction Rules (RAPIER) [49] and Boosted Wrapper Induction (BWI) [50] are two other examples of learning-based information extractors. An example of information extraction template for DISCOTEX approach is presented in Fig. 3.12.

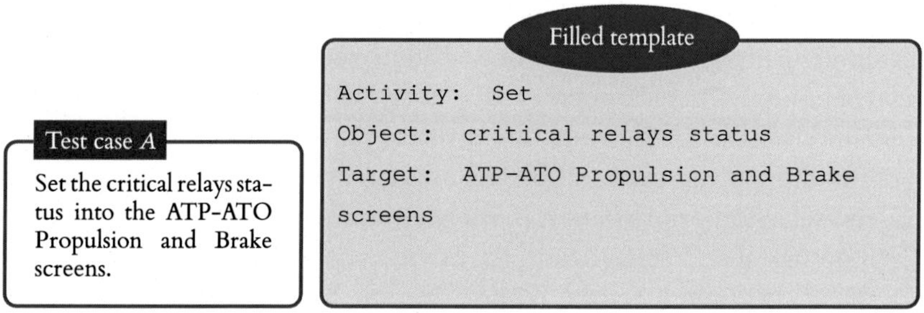

Figure 3.12 An example information extraction template for the DISCOTEX approach. Source: Authors' own contribution.

3.2. Text transformation and representation

Besides the advantages of utilizing the mentioned text analytics methods from the previous sections, the required time and effort for deploying them in the industry need to be considered as well. As we presented in Chapter 2, the length of a natural text document in a typical production environment can vary. It can be a short table or a large test analysis report. Due to the various sizes, quality, and required effort for applying the analytic methods, the usage of transforming a natural text document to an array has received a great deal of attention. Transforming a natural text document to numbers and vectors has two main advantages: (1) it provides a compatible input for most machine learning models and (2) it provides meaningful analytics for the initial text document [51]. In fact, the transformation provides the ability to represent a word using its corresponding indexes and position in a dictionary from a larger text document.

Shortly said, for text representation and transformation, we need to measure the similarity distances between input text (words, sentences, paragraphs, or documents), where if two text documents have a similar meaning they are closer together, and those documents that are different are further apart [51]. Using text similarity as distance provides the opportunity for applying clustering and classification approaches. In the upcoming paragraphs, we review some of the existing solutions for measuring the similarity distances between natural text input.

3.2.1 String distances

String distance, which is also known as the string similarity metric, is one of the simplest approaches to perform approximate string matching using functions that measure the distance between pairs of strings.

There are various functions that provide distance values to identify how (dis)similar pairs of text are from one another, such as Levenshtein, Jaccard, and Hamming. These functions have been widely used in the literature to identify similarities between test artifacts [52–55], and different studies analyzed the specific trade-off between different functions being used for, e.g., test selection prioritization [56] or test suite minimization [57].

Choosing the best function to extract test information is context-dependent. In some literature reports, specific functions result in a better average percentage of faults detected (APFD) [56]. In contrast, other studies reported very little difference when comparing reduction results, such as the test coverage ratio [52,53,57].

Consequently, practitioners should understand the benefits and drawbacks of different functions to choose the most suitable one for their context. To explain those trade-offs, we focus on two categories of string distance measures based on, respectively, the edit operations to transform one string into another and the common tokens between both strings. Edit distance measures quantify the dissimilarity between two strings based on the minimal number of operations required to transform one string into the other. In other words, the measure is based on the number of insertions, deletions, or substitutions of characters needed to obtain two equal strings [56]. Edit distances have been widely applied to a variety of cases, such as spell checkers and DNA sequencing [58], and also to identifying similarities between test inputs [56] and test sequences [55]. Being the most commonly used, the term Levenshtein distance is often utilized interchangeably with edit distance. The edit distance metrics vary in how the set of string operations is used or weighted. For instance, while the Levenshtein distance [59] equally counts the insertion, deletion, and substitution operations, the Jaro distances give a higher rating to strings that match at the beginning for a chosen length. Conversely, other variations such as the Hamming distance [60] are limited to measuring distances between strings of the same length. In turn, token-based distances quantify the number of similar sub-strings of length q, also referred to as q-grams, between two strings. As an example, token-based distances can measure similarity based on phonemes, syllables, letters, or entire words depending on the value chosen for q. The token-based metrics vary in how they count the overlap between those different tokens. For instance, the Jaccard index measures the overlap between the sets of q-grams obtained from two strings, whereas the cosine distance considers similarities between feature vectors extracted from those strings (e.g., topics or words). When applied to diversity-based testing, token-based distances perform reasonably well in identifying subsets of diverse tests that reveal different faults [52,61]. One of the main drawbacks is efficiency, due to the costs of creating the q-grams and then comparing their pairwise similarity. Miranda et al. apply the technique of Shingling and Minhashing to improve the efficiency of token-based techniques by avoiding pairwise comparison of tests and, instead, comparing the entire test suite [61].

3.2.2 Normalized compression distance

In contrast to their simplicity and effectiveness, string distance is limited to textual data. Since tests can be represented by many types of data (e.g., numeric, images, audio), more generic metrics that convey similarity yield more flexibility to the application of diversity-based testing to a variety of domains. Such metrics are based on the information distance between two entities, where the similarity between both entities is the length of the shortest program that converts one entity into another.

Even though the information distance is a universal measure of similarity [62], it is, in practice, generally not feasible to be calculated [63]. Therefore, Cilibrasi and Vitanyi proposed the normalized compression distance (NCD), which is an approximation of such distance based on the length of the compressed entities x and y. Their approach verifies how similar both entities are by applying a compression algorithm C in entities x and y separately and comparing its length to the same compression on the concatenation of both entities [64]:

$$NCD(x, y) = \frac{C(xy) - min\{C(x), C(y)\}}{max\{C(x), C(y)\}}. \tag{3.1}$$

NCD has been used in a variety of applications, including software testing [52,54,65]. In fact, recent evidence shows that it is among the best candidates for black box test prioritization [66]. However, NCD is computationally expensive, such that its application in large test suites becomes prohibitive [65]. Feldt et al. propose the usage of the NCD applied to multisets, instead of pairwise comparison, to overcome such prohibitive scenarios [65]. Furthermore, the choice of compressor C may have an impact on the distance values. Different compressors affect various parameters, such as throughput, compression/decompression speed, and memory. Different compressors have been used and compared in a variety of domains, such as image processing [67] and genome data sequencing [68].

3.3. Vectorization

Studies show that machine learning algorithms perform generally better on numeric inputs such as a two-dimensional array where the rows present samples and the features are embedded in the columns [51]. However, as stated before, for employing machine learning models for text analysis purposes, the text documents need to be transformed into vector representations. This process is called vectorization, which can be considered as a key element for operating the new artificial intelligence and also machine learning algorithms. As vectorization has a wide range of applications it can also be defined in different ways.

Definition 3.2. The process of transforming the input data (e.g., image, text) into a vector representation is called vectorization, which is an essential first step toward operating the artificial intelligence and machine learning algorithms [51].

Vectorization is a powerful process in scientific computing where huge chunks of data need to be processed efficiently.

In mathematics, vectorization is a linear transformation of an $m \times n$ matrix A that converts it into a column vector. In other words, $vec(A)$ is the $mn \times 1$ column vector achieved by accumulating the columns of the matrix A on top of one another [69]:

$$vec(A) = [a_{1,1,\dots}, a_{m,1}, a_{1,2}, \dots, a_{m,2}, \dots, a_{1,n}, \dots, a_{m,n}]^T,$$

where a_{ij} is $A(ij)$ and ^{T} is the transpose of a matrix A. Thus vectorization between the matrices and vectors in a vector space can be represented as follows:

$$\mathbf{R}^{m \times n} := \mathbf{R}^m \otimes \mathbf{R}^n \cong \mathbf{R}^{mn}.$$

For instance, for matrix $A_{(2 \times 2)} = \begin{bmatrix} a & b \\ c & d \end{bmatrix}$, the vectorization is

$$vec(A) = \begin{bmatrix} a \\ c \\ b \\ d \end{bmatrix}.$$

We need to consider that the connection between the vectorization of A and the vectorization of its transpose is given by the commutation matrix.[3]

As stated earlier in this section, there is a wide range of applications for vectorization such as image tracing, array programming,[4] language–aware analysis, and also automatic vectorization (in parallel computing).

3.3.1 Text vectorization

Text vectorization, also known as word embeddings and word vectorization, is generally referred to as the feature extraction process of converting text into meaningful vectors (sequences of numbers). Text vectorization can be utilized to represent text for the artificial intelligence/machine learning algorithms in order to solve natural language processing tasks (e.g., compute similar words, text classifications, and document clustering) in a more efficient way [71].

There are several methods for text vectorization, ranging from simple matrix-based approaches to neural networks. However, the proper vectorization method for text vectorization is highly dependent on the application. In the following paragraphs, we provide an overview of some of the most applicable text vectorization methods, where each method is described along with its advantages, disadvantages, and potential applications.

- **Term frequency.** Term frequency (TF), also known as *binary term frequency*, measures the frequency of a presence or absence (frequency of 0) of a word W in the corresponding document D [72]:

$$TF = \frac{appearance\ of\ W\ in\ document\ D}{the\ total\ number\ of\ words\ in\ document\ D}. \qquad (3.2)$$

As we can see in Eq. (3.2), TF represents the ratio of a word's appearance in a document to the total number of words in an entire document.

One test step from the presented test specification in Table 2.3 is employed for measuring the TF for each word which is summarized in Table 3.1. As we can see in Table 3.1, the total number of words in the entire text is equal to 12, where just the unique words are presented in

---

[3] The commutation matrix is used for transforming the vectorized form of a matrix into the vectorized form of its transpose [70].

[4] In array programming, vectorization is the process of converting an algorithm from operating on a single value at a time to operating on a set of values (vector) at a time.

Table 3.1 Measuring the TF for one test step from the presented test case in Table 2.3.

Document		
Text	**Words**	**TF**
Set the critical relays status into the ATP-ATO Propulsion and Brake screens.	Set	1/12
	the	2/12
	critical	1/12
	relays	1/12
	status	1/12
	into	1/12
	ATP-ATO	1/12
	Propulsion	1/12
	and	1/12
	Brake	1/12
	screens	1/12
The total number of words in the document	12	

the word column. The TF is measured for each word which shows the ratio of appearance of each word. Moreover, *ATP-ATO* is detected as one word since they are joined via a hyphen.

Although the TF has shown good performance for most Bayesian models, it might be the case that the most frequent words (e.g., grammatical articles, "of," "and") are not always the most informative and significant words [73,74].

- **Inverse document frequency (IDF).** In order to solve the main mentioned limitation of the TF, the IDF of each word was proposed. IDF measures the importance of a word W in document D by adding a weight to each word based on its frequency in the corpus D [75]:

$$IDF = log_2 \left(\frac{N}{D(W+1)} \right), \qquad (3.3)$$

where $D(W)$ is the number of documents that contain term W and N is the total number of documents in corpus D.

- **TF-IDF.** TF-IDF is simply the product of TF and IDF, which adds more weight to the word that is rare in the corpus and thereby in all the documents [76].

In other words, the TF-IDF provides more importance to the word W if it appears more frequently in document D, which can be calculated

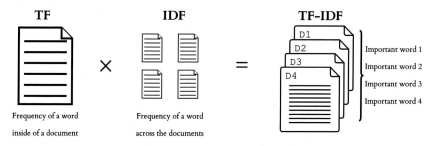

Figure 3.13 Representation of the TF-IDF calculation for the individual words of a text. Source: Authors' own contribution.

as follows:

$$TF - IDF = TF(W, D) * IDF(W, D). \qquad (3.4)$$

In fact, if the word W is very common and appears in many documents, TF-IDF will approach 0; otherwise, it will approach 1. Via measuring the TF-IDF, the text in different documents (document $D1$ and $D2$) will be represented as a TF-IDF vector. The dimension of a TF-IDF vector is equal to the vocabulary words. Moreover, the value corresponding to each word indicates the importance of that word in a particular document [77]. As we can see in Fig. 3.13, running the TF-IDF model can be computationally expensive especially for a large vocabulary. However, the main disadvantage of the TF-IDF is the lack of ability for detecting the semantic meaning of words. For instance, *Set* and *Put* are synonyms, but the TF-IDF model is not able to detect this.

Additionally, employing the TF-IDF model also requires a normalization step. In order to scale the obtained values by the TF-IDF model between 0 and 1, we need to normalize the product of TF and IDF, which can be performed via $L1$ and $L2$ normalization as follows:

- **L1 normalization.**[5] Each element in a vector (various TF-IDF values of a sentence) is divided by the sum of absolute values of all elements [78].
- **L2 normalization.** Each vector is divided by the length of the vector [78].
- **Bag of words TF.** The bag of words TF measures the occurrence of words within a document [79]. In the bag of words model, a text is

[5] Also known as the taxicab norm or the Manhattan norm.

represented as the bag of its words, disregarding grammar, the vocabulary of known words, and even word order measurement, but keeping multiplicity [79,80].

The bag of words model can be trained in the following two different ways:

- **Continuous bag of words (CBoW).** CBoW tries to predict the vector representation of a center/target word based on a window of context words. The architecture of the CBoW model is shown in Fig. 3.14. As we can see, the CBoW model aims to predict the current target word (the center word in Fig. 3.14) based on the source context (surrounding in Fig. 3.14) words [81].

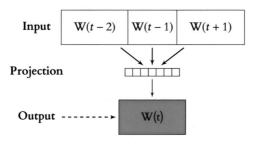

Figure 3.14 The structure of the continuous bag of words (CBoW) model. Source: Mikolov et al. [81].

In order to get a better overview of the CBoW model, let us review the presented sentence (test step example in Table 2.3) again:

> *"Set the critical relays status into the ATP-ATO Propulsion and Brake screens."*

The above-provided example can be pairs of (context–window, target–word), where if we consider a context window of size 2, the following selected examples can be achieved:

1. ([critical, status], relays),
2. ([the, critical], status),
3. ([Propulsion, Brake], screens).

In fact, the CBoW model aims to predict the target–word based on the context–window words [81].

- **Distributed bag of words (DBoW).** DBoW does not focus on the context words in the input, where it takes the document ID as the input and tries to predict randomly sampled words from the document [82]. Fig. 3.15 shows the structure of a DBoW model.

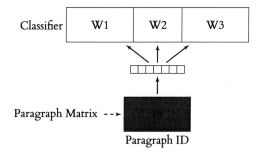

Figure 3.15 The structure of the distributed bag of words (DBoW) model. Source: Le and Mikolov [83].

Assume that the DBoW model tries to learn by predicting two sampled words from the presented test step example in Table 2.3. Thus, in order to learn the document vector, two words are sampled from:
1. W_1: Set,
2. W_1: the,
3. W_4: critical,
4. W_5: relays.

As mentioned before, the DBoW model ignores the context words in the input, but it forces the model to predict words randomly sampled from the paragraph in the output and a paragraph ID [82]. Moreover, the paragraph matrix in Fig. 3.15 is the matrix where each column represents the vector of a paragraph. Matrix D has the embeddings for "seen" paragraphs for words. For "unseen" paragraphs, the model is again run by gradient descent to derive a document vector [82,83]. For instance, given a sentence including three words "[W1 W2 W3]" (see Fig. 3.15), two words are sampled from it.

- **Skip-gram (SG).** SG tries to find the most closely related words for a given word. SG also predicts the context word for a given target word, which can be considered as a reverse of the CBoW model (see Fig. 3.14). As we can see in Fig. 3.16, in the SG model, the target word is input while context words are the expected output.

Let us review the presented sentence (test step example in Table 2.3) again:

> *"Set the critical relays status into the ATP-ATO Propulsion and Brake screens."*

For the above example, the word "*critical*" will be given and SG tries to predict words "*Set, status*" at positions -2 and -1, respectively, assuming that *critical* is at position 0. We need to consider that SG does

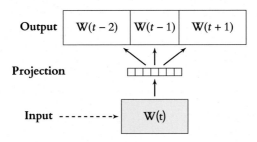

Figure 3.16 The structure of the skip-gram (SG) model. Source: Mikolov et al. [81].

not predict common or stop words, e.g., grammatical articles, "of", "and" [81].

All above-mentioned vectorization models are able to deal with the input in the text form. However, sometimes, the input data might be numerical data, categorical data, or time-series data. In order to vectorize different types of data, e.g., categorical data, the data needs to be converted to a numerical form. Categorical data is a collection of information that is divided into groups such as a month of birth or state of residence variables [84]. Generally, the categorical variable needs to be converted based on the application.

- **One-hot encoding.** One-hot encoding is a type of representation that converts the categorical data variables to machine-readable format [85].

During the one-hot encoding process, the value of 0 will be assigned to all elements in a vector. However, there is an exception just for one element, which has a value of 1 and indicates a category of an element. In the case of encoding text segments using one-hot encoding, there are two possibilities depending on the use. In both cases, we can say that columns correspond to individual words from the dictionary. In the first variant, we can encode the entire segment in one row, but we lose the ordering of words, similar to the bag of words approach; this concept is illustrated in Table 3.2. In the second approach, we keep the correct sequence of words by encoding words one by one and thus representing every text segment by a matrix.

One-hot encoding requires less effort for the implementation and the output can be more easily interpreted compared to other similar methods. However, employing one-hot encoding for a high-dimensional sparse matrix representation can be slower and more memory-expensive than alternative approaches.

Table 3.2 One-hot encoded data representations of "Set the critical relays status into the ATP-ATO Propulsion and Brake screens" and "Set all relays status critical."

Vocabulary						One-hot encoding							
	and	ATP-ATO	all	Brake	critical	into	Propulsion	relays	screens	Set	status	the
Document 1	1	1	0	1	1	1	1	1	1	1	1	1
Document 2	0	0	1	0	1	0	0	1	0	1	1	0

3.3.2 Machine learning

As highlighted earlier in this chapter, the main drawbacks of the mentioned old text analytics methods are their inability to handle large volumes of raw data, low accuracy, and also the self-training process. With the advent of new technology, machine learning algorithms were used to reduce the mentioned limitations. Contrary to the traditional programming rules, machine learning algorithms can learn and improve by themselves by studying high volumes of available data. Therefore, very high volumes of raw data alone can teach algorithms to create better computing models [86].

Before we jump into the details of the machine learning process, let us clarify how the available data (regardless of type) can be partitioned, as a first step in developing any machine learning model.

Figure 3.17 An overview of partitioning data into training, validation, and testing sets.

The input data to a machine learning model must be divided into multiple datasets which will be utilized later in different stages of the model creation. Fig. 3.17 provides an overview of partitioning the input data into the following datasets:

1. **Training set.** The training set is a partition of the original dataset used to fit the model. The machine learning model will learn from this dataset.
2. **Validation set.** The validation set is a partition of the original dataset used to provide an evaluation of a model fit on the training dataset.
3. **Test set.** The test set, also known as a holdout set, is a partition of the original dataset used to provide some critical standards to evaluate the *final model fit* on the training dataset.

Dividing the data into the mentioned partitions is directly related to the data size, quality, machine learning model, and application; however, some common ratios which can be used for splitting the original dataset are:

- 80% training, 10% validation, 10% test;
- 70% training, 15% validation, 15% test;
- 60% training, 20% validation, 20% test.

As we can see in the above ratios and also in Fig. 3.17, the training set should always be smaller than the test set. The main idea behind this segmentation is to ensure a more accurate calculation of model performance.

On the other hand, this segmentation can help us speed up our training, due to the smaller size of the used data, and make the final results more reliable [87]. However, it might be the case that we just need to split the original dataset into training and testing sets, so the proposed validation set can be removed. Partitioning the original dataset in a proper way and ratio, knowing which machine learning approach will be employed for solving a problem is required in advance. Machine learning approaches can generally be classified into three major categories as shown in Fig. 3.18:

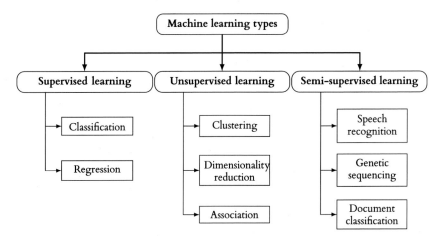

Figure 3.18 The three main categories of machine learning approaches.

1. **Supervised learning.** Supervised learning is a type of machine learning approach that requires the availability of some annotated (labeled) data. The task of supervised learning can be described as the creation of a mapping of the features X (also called input variables) and labels Y (also known as output variables) [88]. As the exact mapping function is often impossible or very difficult to determine, we need to approximate the mapping function. The training set, validation set, and test set in the previous paragraphs need to be utilized if we are using a supervised learning approach for solving a problem. In supervised learning, we can guess the correct answer; therefore, supervised learning problems are further grouped into regression and classification problems [89].

2. **Unsupervised learning.** Unsupervised learning is a good solution when just input data is known and both output data and the mapping function are unknown. In unsupervised learning, a machine learning algorithm tries to find a function that discovers relationships in the in-

put data. The main advantage of unsupervised learning is the ability to solve a problem that humans might find insurmountable due to either scale or biases. Clustering, dimensionality reduction, and association are the main categories of unsupervised learning [90,91]. The training set and test set should be utilized if we are using an unsupervised learning approach.

3. **Semi-supervised learning.** Semi-supervised learning is a combination of supervised and unsupervised learning in terms of labeled data samples, where we have a small portion of labeled examples and a large number of unlabeled samples. In semi-supervised learning, the model needs to learn and make predictions on new examples. Reinforcement learning and data cleaning are two applications of semi-supervised learning.

As shown in Fig. 3.18, there are several methods and sub-disciplines for each of the mentioned machine learning-based approaches. In the upcoming chapters, we provide several applications, where different machine learning approaches are utilized for solving industrial problems. Knowing the different data segmentation and machine learning approaches, we can analyze the process of implementing a machine learning solution. In Fig. 3.19 we demonstrate a schematic overview of a machine learning-based process; in summary, a machine learning algorithm utilizes three main steps for analyzing raw data, where those steps can be completely unique or part of the traditional solutions.

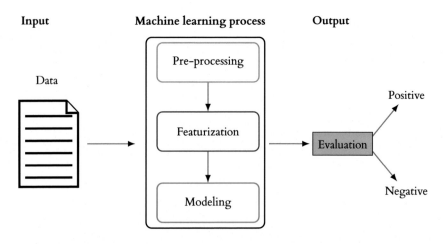

Figure 3.19 A schematic diagram of a machine learning-based approach for text mining.

1. **Pre-processing.** Pre-processing has a significant impact on the generalization performance of supervised machine learning algorithms [92]; thus, the input data need to be pre-processed in an early stage of using any machine learning-based model. Data pre-processing can be performed in several ways, e.g., data cleaning, data integration, normalization, and reduction. However, based on the data type, size, and quality, one or more of the mentioned data pre-processing methods need to be applied to the raw data.

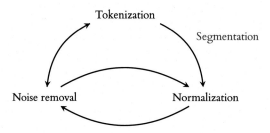

Figure 3.20 A framework of some of the text data pre-processing approaches.

Fig. 3.20 illustrates an overview of some of the most common text data pre-processing approaches, where each step can be replaced or skipped based on the data size, quality, and application. Since the main application of the proposed artificial intelligence-based solution in this book is text mining, we will focus more on the data pre-processing methods that are applicable to natural text documents, such as tokenization. In a tokenization process, a long string of text is split into smaller pieces which are called tokens. There are several ways for performing tokenization, such as tokenization of text into sentences, tokenization of sentences into words, or tokenization of sentences using regular expressions. Further data processing is generally performed after a piece of text has been appropriately tokenized. Tokenization can also refer to text segmentation or lexical analysis. An unsupervised text tokenizer is usually embedded for neural network-based text generation systems (e.g., SBERT algorithm). However, for the distance-based and compression-based algorithms, we need to employ tokenization separately as the first step. The main use of tokenization is to identify the meaningful keywords [93] and therefore it can be considered an inseparable part of modern language processing. The tokens help in understanding the context of the natural language processing models by interpreting the meaning of the text via analyzing the sequence of the words.

In order to get a better understanding of the tokenization concept, the presented test specification in Table 2.3 will be tokenized using Python. Table 3.3 presents the tokenized version, where the "Action" and "Expected result" columns are extracted and utilized from Table 2.3 for the tokenization process.

Table 3.3 The tokenized version of the presented test case in Table 2.3, using the "Action" and "Expected result" columns.

['1', 'set', 'dt1', 'cab', 'to', 'active', 'verify', 'that', 'the', 'critical', 'relays', 'status', 'on', 'car', 'level', 'is', 'displaying', 'on', 'vdu', '.', 'set', 'the', 'critical', 'relays', 'status', 'into', 'the', 'atp', 'ato', 'propulsion', 'and', 'brake', 'screens', '.', '2', 'set', 'no', 'critical', 'relays', 'status', 'in', 'atp', 'ato', ',', 'propulsion', 'and', 'brake', 'screens', '.', 'verify', 'that', 'the', 'critical', 'relays', 'status', 'on', 'car', 'level', 'is', 'not', 'displaying', 'on', 'vdu', '.', '3', 'repeat', 'the', 'above', 'steps', 'for', 'dt2', 'cab']

Furthermore, Fig. 3.21 shows the similarities and changes between the tokenized and original versions of the same test case which has been presented in Table 3.3 and Table 2.3, using the Levenshtein equality. As we can see, the original text and the tokenized version are 78.69% common with 21.31% of differences. Moreover, the minor changes presented in Fig. 3.21 can be considered as the capitalization and word spacing. Hereof, we decide to pre-process the raw data employing the most common tokenization approach as it is efficient, can be implemented in multiple languages, and preserves the non-language artifacts well, such as names of modules. In fact, the tokenization process removes the majority of punctuation and converts all text to lowercase.

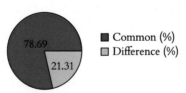

Figure 3.21 Text comparison between the original and tokenized versions of the presented test case in Table 2.3 and Table 3.3, using the Levenshtein equality.

Normalization generally refers to a series of related tasks meant to put all text on a level playing field: converting all text to the same case (upper or lower), removing punctuation, converting numbers to their word equivalents, and so on. Normalization puts all words on equal footing and allows processing to proceed uniformly. Noise removal continues the substitution tasks of the presented framework in Fig. 3.20, which is a much more task-specific section of the framework. As you can imagine, the boundary between noise removal and data collection and assembly is a fuzzy one, and as such, some noise removal must take place before other pre-processing steps. For example, any text required from a JSON structure would obviously need to be removed prior to tokenization. Lower casing, removing special characters, contraction expansion, removing stop words, correcting spelling, stemming, and lemmatization are other solutions for data pre-processing.

2. **Featurization.** Featurization generally refers to methods that convert varied forms of data (variables) to numerical data (features) which can be utilized for machine learning algorithms. In this book, we use the featurization terminology in order to cover its other sub-disciplines such as feature selection, feature extraction, feature engineering, and also feature learning. Featurization in a machine learning process might include all of the mentioned sub-disciplines or sometimes we just need to apply one of them. However, the differences between the mentioned sub-disciplines need to be considered before we select a proper approach for featurization. Feature extraction is a proper approach when the original data is very different and cannot be used as raw data. However, feature engineering is pre-processing the raw data into more meaningful features. Feature engineering is a vital step for text mining especially on the unstructured data, where we always need to convert the text into a numeric representation that can be read as input by different machine learning algorithms. Featurization facilitates the speed of learning and generalization steps in the machine learning process. Bag of words (see Figs. 3.14 and 3.15) and TF-IDF (see Fig. 3.13) can be mentioned as the most popular methods of featurization.

3. **Modeling.** Modeling is a process of training various statistical and probabilistic techniques to predict the labels from the features, tuning them for the applications and validating them on testing dataset [94]. Based on the final application, different approaches can be employed for the modeling process shown in Fig. 3.19, such as support vector machines, decision tree, Bayesian networks, maximum entropy, conditional random field, neural networks, and also deep learning-based models.

After implementing the mentioned process in Fig. 3.19, the machine learning model will provide some outputs, generally in the form of a probability, a class, or clusters. However, since employing machine learning models in industries is still an expensive activity, we need to monitor how effective the model is based on some metric which explains the performance of a machine learning model.

The performance metric for evaluating the performance of the machine learning solutions should be selected carefully and properly. Selecting the wrong performance metric might complicate the interpretation of the output, which was one of the big obstacles that we faced during our research. In Table 3.4 we summarize some of the most popular and application metrics for evaluating the performance of a machine learning model. Later in this book, the mentioned performance metrics in Table 3.4 are utilized for the conducted industrial case studies.

Table 3.4 Some popular evaluation metrics in machine learning.

Metric	Definition	Application
NMI	Measures the normalized mutual information (0: no mutual information; 1: perfect correlation) between two partitions	Clustering
AMI	Measures the adjusted mutual information between two partitions	Clustering
ARI	Stands for adjusted rand index, which measures the similarity between two data partitions, where it is adjusted for the chance grouping of elements	Clustering
Accuracy	Measures how often the algorithm classifies a data point correctly on a balanced dataset	Classification
Precision	Measures the proportion of positive identifications that are actually correct	Classification/ clustering
Recall	Measures the ability of a machine learning model to find all the relevant cases within a dataset	Classification/ clustering
F1-score	Shows the harmonic mean of precision and recall and can be employed for balanced and imbalanced datasets	Classification/ clustering
ROC	Stands for receiver operating characteristic, which is a curve that shows the performance of a classification model at all classification thresholds. ROC is a proper measurement, especially for imbalanced datasets	Imbalanced classification
AUC	Stands for area under the curve, which is the measure of the ability of a classifier to distinguish between classes and is used as a summary of the ROC curve	Imbalanced classification

It might be the case that the utilized machine learning model provides satisfying results when evaluated using a metric such as accuracy on an imbalanced dataset; however, the same model might provide a poor result when it is evaluated against other metrics, e.g., F1-score or AUC.

In order to get a better understanding of the presented steps for utilizing a machine learning-based approach in Fig. 3.19, we introduce and describe some models which are later employed in the provided case studies. Moreover, since this book tries to provide an implementation guideline for experts in industries, we added some potential algorithms to each model which easily can be reused. Although the proposed models and solutions in the upcoming paragraphs mainly focus on applications in software testing, by changing some of the steps in the original pipelines we can utilize them for other applications, such as social media analysis and image processing.

3.3.3 Neural word embeddings

Natural language processing is an intersection between machine learning and artificial intelligence which is one of the most significant progressions in the text analytics domain. Recently, word embeddings are imprinted inside of the advanced neural architectures. As explained before, word embedding (which is also known as text vectorization, semantic vector space, vector representation, and word feature vector) represents a word as a vector of numeric values.

Fig. 3.22 illustrates an example of a neural system architecture of word embeddings, which is proposed by Thanaki [95]. As we can see in Fig. 3.22, the text document should be pre-processed using the pre-processing techniques presented in this chapter. Later, the word vectors are initialized with pre-trained word representations from one of the three models: PV-DBoW (see Fig. 3.15), SG (see Fig. 3.16), or CBoW (see Fig. 3.14). As explained before, the CBoW predicts the vector representation of center (target) words based on a window of context words. Also, SG predicts the vector representation of a window of context words based on center (target) words. Once we have the embedded vectors for each word, we are able to use them for text analysis purposes. In summary, the neural network word embedding models will convert the text into a vector representation. For the featurization process, the model allows neural networks to learn the features themselves. Now the input is a feature vector of the text and the output is expected to be some high-level semantic information such as classification. Finally, the words are going to be classified as "positive" or "negative."

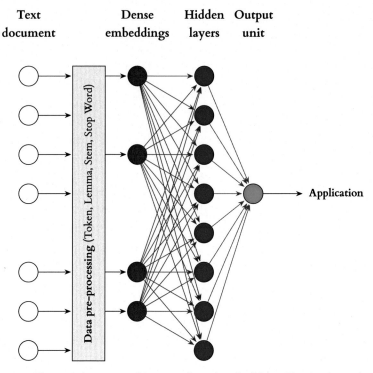

Figure 3.22 The neural system architecture of word embeddings. The words need to be pre-processed first using tokenization, stemming, lemmatization, and/or stop word removal. Source: Thanaki [95].

Since word embedding is capable of capturing the context of a word in a document, semantic and syntactic similarity, and relations with other words, it has a wide range of applications. There are several proposed implementations of the term word embedding, where the word-to-vector (Word2Vec) model is one of the most popular techniques to learn word embeddings which provides an embedded representation of words. Word2Vec starts with one representation of all words in the corpus and trains a neural network (with one hidden layer) on a very large corpus of data. The Word2Vec model was developed in 2013 by Tomas Mikolov [96].

In 2014, the document-to-vector (Doc2Vec) model was proposed by Le and Mikolov [83]. Doc2Vec has excellent scalability and it also covers the gaps of previous approaches where the semantics of the words were ignored. Another of its advantages is that it learns from unlabeled data, meaning that it is applicable for tasks that do not have enough labeled data, which is often the case in industrial applications. Doc2Vec is also independent of the language and can be applied to most languages with minimal modification. The goal of Doc2Vec is to create a fixed-length numeric representation of a document, regardless of its length. Indeed, for each document, Doc2Vec provides an n-dimensional vector, in which each dimension can be interpreted as a feature. Overall in this book, we use paragraph vectors (a PyTorch implementation of Doc2Vec) with a DBoW model which uses single-layer neural networks to predict whether a word is contained in a given text document. In fact, the Doc2Vec model is employed in this book for analyzing different test artifacts which have a text format such as requirements specifications and test specifications.

3.3.4 Log vectorization

One of the most significant recent advances in word embeddings is in analyzing both structured and unstructured text data. Although a requirement or test specification might have not been structured in a pre-defined manner, some of the machine-generated reports such as log files have a pre-defined format. It is obvious that the structured text can easily be digested by the natural language processing models, whereas an unstructured text might not. Most of the advanced natural language processing techniques can simply utilize a bag of words or similar model for this purpose. However, the complexity of the natural text (it can be a combination of both structured and unstructured text) might require more complicated approaches which attempt to pull out deeper language structures like parts of speech. A log report generally provides detailed event audit information in a format that minimizes the report's impact on system resources. An example of structured data in a log file can be tester ID, data, and results, where the related unstructured data might be the text of the failure report. Log representation, which converts unstructured texts to structured vectors or matrices, serves as the first step towards automated log analysis. However, the current log representation methods neither represent domain-specific semantic information of logs nor handle the out-of-vocabulary words of new types of logs at runtime [97].

As explained earlier, representing documents numerically gives us the ability to perform meaningful analytics and also creates the instances in which machine learning algorithms operate. In text analysis, instances are entire documents or utterances, which can vary in length from quotes or tweets to entire books, but whose vectors are always of a uniform length. Each property of the vector representation is a feature. For text, features represent attributes and properties of documents including its content as

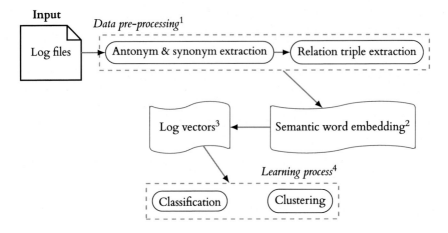

Figure 3.23 The customized system architecture of the Log2Vec model. Source: Liu et al. [97].

well as meta-attributes, such as document length, author, source, and publication date. When considered together, the features of a document describe a multidimensional feature space on which machine learning methods can be applied [51]. In this regard, Log2Vec is a semantic-aware representation framework for log analysis which was proposed by Meng et al. [97] in 2020. Log2Vec combines a log-specific word embedding method to accurately extract the semantic information of logs. In Fig. 3.23 we present a customized version of the Log2Vec model which is mapped with the conducted industrial case studies in this book. For running the presented model for log analysis, we need to follow up the following steps:

1. The gathered log files should be entered as input to the Log2Vec model.
2. Log2Vec uses a data pre-processing pipeline, where the first step is antonym and synonym extraction. Antonyms indicate the words which have opposite meanings (e.g., up and down) and synonyms are words that have similar meanings (e.g., down and below). The main reason for employing antonym and synonym extraction is to reduce the total number of irrelevant words and avoid duplication. Relation triple extraction, which is shown in Fig. 3.23, is utilized for the same purpose but it acts differently compared to antonym and synonym extraction. Indeed, relation triple extraction will extract the words which occur together (e.g., interface, changed, state).
3. The output after performing data pre-processing is then converted to vectors. This process will be managed in the semantic word embedding, which is highlighted as step 2 in Fig. 3.23.

4. The output from step 2 is a set of log vectors that will be utilized for classification or clustering purposes.
5. Different classification methods can be used in this step (e.g., neural network-based approaches or even linear classification models such as SVM).
6. The output from the previous step is a number of classes which include the log files. The obtained classes can be employed for different test optimization purposes such as troubleshooting activities.

In summary, if two log files end up in the same classes or clusters, they have required the same troubleshooting activity. In this book, we employ and evaluate Log2Vec via conducting an industrial case study as a novel approach to classify similar logs which need the same troubleshooting.

3.3.5 Code vectorization

Generally, for testing a software product, we might end up having a large set of test cases (both test specifications and test scripts). Executing the test cases without any particular order can directly impact the costs and also deadlines. In order to execute test cases in a more efficient way, we need to identify their relations in an early stage of the testing process. Analyzing a large set of the generated test scripts manually is a time- and resource-consuming process which requires knowledge in both programming and testing. Since the main goal of this book is to provide a solution for the vectorization of different test artifacts, we introduce, apply, and evaluate another neural model for code embeddings. In 2018, Alon et al. [98] presented a neural model for representing snippets of code as continuously distributed vectors called code embeddings.

The main idea was to represent a code snippet as a single fixed-length code vector, which can be used to predict the semantic properties of the snippet. This is performed by decomposing code into a collection of paths in its abstract syntax tree and learning the atomic representation of each path simultaneously with learning how to aggregate a set of them. Alon et al. [98] demonstrate the effectiveness of the Code2Vec approach by using it to predict a method's name from the vector representation of its body. Code2Vec is already evaluated by training a model on a dataset of $14M$ methods. It seems that the code vectors model trained on this dataset can predict method names from files that were completely unobserved during training. Comparing previous techniques over the same dataset, Code2Vec obtains a relative improvement of over 75%, being the first to successfully predict method names based on a large cross-project corpus. In Fig. 3.24

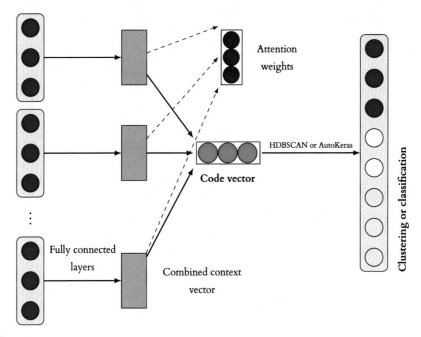

Figure 3.24 Customized version of the neural system architecture of code embeddings. Source: Alon et al. [98].

we present a customized version of the Code2Vec model. For running the presented model in Fig. 3.24 for code analysis, we need to follow the following steps:

1. test script acquisition;
2. test script ground truth creation by manual annotation (for supervised learning);
3. test script pre-processing:
   a. unifying the test script folder and name structure,
   b. cleaning up the test scripts by removing the metadata and incompatible comments;
4. acquiring the pre-trained model for Code2Vec;
5. generating embeddings using Code2Vec based on the pre-trained model;
6. splitting the dataset into training and testing datasets;
7. running AutoKeras to find the best fit model for the classification or using HDBSCAN for the clustering;
8. measuring the fitness of the found model.

3.4. Imbalanced learning

At a certain point, we realized that classification and clustering of the test artifacts are mainly two final solutions for test optimization purposes. Although using the proposed solutions for the vectorization of the text, log and code can help us to have a better overview of the test artifacts, we might face another problem that cannot be solved by the vectorization. One of the critical challenges in real-world industrial settings. especially in classification, is having an imbalanced dataset. For instance, we may aim to divide all test cases into two classes: (1) dependent test cases and (2) independent test cases. In this situation, we have a 2-class (binary) classification problem where one class (the minority class) to be classified is significantly less represented than the other (the majority class). Let us assume that we have 50 test cases where a total of 45 test cases are labeled as independent and the remaining 5 test cases are labeled as dependent test cases (see Fig. 3.25).

Figure 3.25 Example of balanced and imbalanced datasets for dividing test cases into depen dent and independent and similar and non-similar classes.

This is an example of an imbalanced dataset, where the imbalance ratio (IR) can be calculated using Eq. (3.5):

$$IR = \frac{Majority_{examples}}{Minority_{examples}}. \tag{3.5}$$

As expressed in Eq. (3.5), the IR is a ratio between the number of samples in the majority class and the number of samples in the minority class [99]. Some researchers consider that a dataset suffers from an imbalance problem if the IR is higher than 3 [99]. However, the degree of imbalance can be divided into the presented groups in Table 3.5.

Table 3.5 The imbalanced dataset range from mild to extreme.

Degree of imbalance	Proportion of minority class
Mild	20–40% of the dataset
Moderate	1–20% of the dataset
Extreme	< 1% of the dataset

Choosing an appropriate approach for dealing with an imbalanced dataset is very important in practice. Data characteristics such as class imbalance and training data size are known to have an intrinsic relationship with classifier performance [100,101].

But, what will happen if we train a classifier with an imbalanced dataset?

The answer is simple: the classifier tends to make a biased learning model that has a poorer predictive accuracy over the minority classes compared to the majority classes [100,101].

But why is this happening?

Well, we need to remember that most classifiers are designed based on the following assumptions:

1. The class distribution in the dataset is relatively balanced.
2. The costs of misclassification are equal for each class.
3. The classification rules that are designed to predict the minority classes tend to be rare, undiscovered, or ignored [100].

Moreover, we might face a class imbalance in multi-class classification problems as well. Choosing an appropriate approach for dealing with an imbalanced dataset is very important in practice. Data characteristics such as class imbalance and training data size have an intrinsic relationship with classifier performance [100]. The remaining discussions will mostly focus on a two-class classification problem. However, most of the proposed solutions for dealing with imbalanced datasets can be employed on both binary and non-binary classification problems.

3.4.1 Random under-sampling

Random under-sampling is one of the techniques that can help us to train a classifier to detect the abnormal class. Random under-sampling involves randomly selecting examples from the majority class and deleting them from the training dataset. In the random under-sampling, the majority class instances are discarded at random until a more balanced distribution is reached [102].

An overview of the random under-sampling approach is illustrated in Fig. 3.26. As we can see, some samples from the majority class (which are highlighted as Label 1 in Fig. 3.26) will be selected to cover the minority class (highlighted as Label 0 in Fig. 3.26).

3.4.2 Random over-sampling

Random over-sampling is another approach for dealing with an imbalanced dataset. Random over-sampling involves randomly selecting examples from

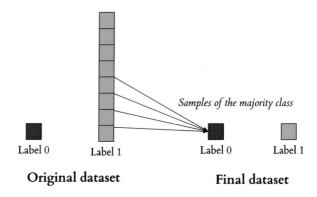

Figure 3.26 A schematic overview of the random under-sampling approach.

the minority class, with replacement, and adding them to the training dataset [103]. An overview of the random over-sampling approach is illustrated in Fig. 3.27. As we can see, some samples from the minority class (which are highlighted as Label 0 in Fig. 3.27) will be copied to the majority class (highlighted as Label 0 in Fig. 3.27).

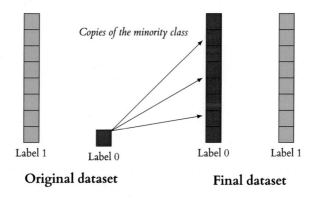

Figure 3.27 A schematic overview of the random over-sampling approach.

3.4.3 Hybrid random sampling

We can also combine under-sampling and over-sampling approaches as a hybrid solution for dealing with imbalanced datasets. First, we need to over-sample the minority class to a high enough degree so that we reduce the imbalance and then further reduce the imbalance by under-sampling the majority classes.

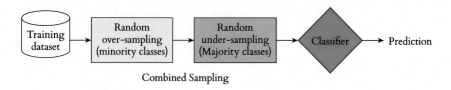

Figure 3.28 A schematic overview of a hybrid sampling model for imbalanced datasets.

A schematic overview of a combined sampling approach is shown in Fig. 3.28. In some cases, a combined (hybrid) approach improves the performance of traditional sampling approaches, which also might improve the generalization performance [101].

3.4.4 Synthetic minority over-sampling technique for balancing data

The *synthetic minority over-sampling technique* (SMOTE) is an over-sampling technique where the synthetic samples are generated for the minority class. This algorithm helps to overcome the over-fitting problem posed by random over-sampling. It focuses on the feature space to generate new instances with the help of interpolation between the positive instances that lie together [104]. Fig. 3.29 depicts an overview of the SMOTE technique, with an original dataset, oversampled one, and a resampled one.

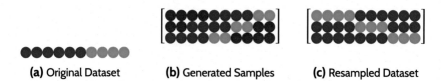

(a) Original Dataset   **(b)** Generated Samples   **(c)** Resampled Dataset

Figure 3.29 A schematic overview of the synthetic minority over-sampling technique (SMOTE). Source: Chawla et al. [104].

3.5. Dimensionality reduction and visualizing machine learning models

As we reviewed up to this point, most of the proposed models for vectorization provide high-dimensional data points as output, which can be employed for classification and clustering purposes.

Definition 3.3. High-dimensional data refers to a dataset where the number of features f (or covariates) can be even larger than the number of observations N [105].

For instance, having a dataset with $f = 6$ features and only $N = 3$ observations is an example of high-dimensional data due to the number of features that are larger than the number of observations.

But why is high-dimensional data a problem?

Well, since we do not have enough observations to train our model, it is almost impossible to find a model that can describe the relationship between the predictor variables and the response variable. In summary, if the number of features in a dataset exceeds the number of observations, we are not able to get a repeatable answer.

The next challenge, especially in industries, is *how can high-dimensional data be handled?*

Generally, there are two popular strategies to deal with high-dimensional data: (1) including fewer features for training a model and (2) employing different regularization methods. In this book, we focus more on the second strategy, since we aim to keep all features.

Dimensionality reduction is the process that reduces the number of input variables (the dimension of the feature set) in a dataset [106]. The traditional techniques for data dimensionality reduction (e.g., low variance in the column values, the high correlation between two columns, principal component analysis [PCA], etc.) usually eliminate those columns that do not add more or new information to the dataset [107]. However, some of the modern techniques (e.g., t-distributed stochastic neighbor embedding [t-SNE] and linear discriminant analysis) require more computational time or are just designed to handle either dimensionality reduction or visualization. On the other hand, visualizing the obtained results can help the experts at industries and also the data scientists to gain more insights into the initial problem and also the achieved results. Visualization also highlights useful information, trends, and outliers. Moreover, data visualization is already considered as a central ingredient of exploratory data analysis, which requires more condensed variables [108]. Since in this book a large industrial dataset needs to be analyzed, we decided to employ two well-known modern techniques which can be utilized for both dimensionality reduction and data visualization simultaneously. Here, uniform manifold approximation and projection (UMAP) and t-SNE are selected for the mentioned purposes.

3.5.1 t-Distributed stochastic neighbor embedding

t-SNE is one of the common statistical methods for visualization of high-dimensional data points. It provides a location in a two- or three-dimensional map to each data point. The t-SNE technique was introduced by Maaten and Hinton [109] in 2008. For a while, t-SNE became very popular in the area of machine learning due to its ability to create compelling two-dimensional "maps" from data with large dimensions [110].

Assume $x_1, x_2, \ldots, x_N$ is a set of high-dimensional data points. As a first step, t-SNE measures the similarity of data point x_j to data point x_i as follows:

$$P_{j|i} = \frac{exp(-||x_i - x_j||^2/2\sigma_i^2)}{\sum_{k \neq i} exp(-||x_i - x_k||^2/2\sigma_i^2)}. \tag{3.6}$$

Note that for nearby data points, $P_{j|i}$ is relatively high, whereas for widely separated data points, $P_{j|i}$ will be almost infinitesimal. By defining $P_{i|i} = 0$, Eq. (3.6) is such that $\sum_j P_{j|i} = 1$ for all i, and in fact for clustering x_i will pick x_j as its neighbor if neighbors are picked in proportion to their probability density.

Let us define y_i as our desired low-dimensional counterparts to x_i. There are many ways to construct the dataset $y_1, \ldots, y_N$ such that y_i and y_j tend to be similar whenever x_i and x_j are similar. For the low-dimensional counterparts such as y_i and y_j of the high-dimensional data points x_i and x_j, it is possible to compute a similar conditional probability, which is denoted as $q_{j|i}$ by Maaten and Hinton. We set the standard deviation of the Gaussian that is employed in the computation of the conditional probabilities $q_{j|i}$ to $\frac{1}{\sqrt{2}}$. Hence, we model the similarity of map point y_j to map point y_i. Let us define the similarity function as Eq. (3.7):

$$q_{j|i} = \frac{exp(-||y_i - y_j||)^2}{\sum_{k \neq i} exp(-||x_i - x_k||)^2}. \tag{3.7}$$

In order to construct the points y_i we can for example take the following steps:
1. Start with some guesses y'_1, y'_N.
2. Define some fitness function to describe how well x_i and y_i match, e.g., Kullback–Leibler divergence.
3. Perform a numerical optimization, e.g., gradient descent method, that gives a good enough fitness, rendering our desired y_i.

Now y_i could be two-dimensional and easy to plot and visualize. Again, since in this book we are only interested in modeling pairwise similarities, we set $q_{i|i} = 0$ as well. Later in this book, we provide more details for the Python implementation and interpretation of the t-SNE techniques, where Kullback–Leibler divergence[6] is utilized for the mapping of the location of each data point.

3.5.2 Uniform manifold approximation and projection

The complexity and diversity of industrial data have forced researchers and data scientists to provide other powerful techniques which can handle large datasets and high-dimensional data without too much difficulty. In this regard, UMAP was proposed by McInnes et al. [111]. UMAP was originally constructed from a theoretical framework based on Riemannian geometry[7] and also algebraic topology [111], which employs an exponential probability distribution which is not normalized in high dimensions. UMAP has some initial similarities with t-SNE, but one main crucial difference is that it removes the need to recompute the similarities between all points in the reduced-dimension dataset at each iteration of the numerical optimization process. This in particular makes it more computationally resilient to the size of the dataset. This renders the algorithm to be optimized using stochastic gradient descent. Let

$$p_{i|j} = e^{-\frac{d(x_i, x_j) - p_i}{\sigma_i}}, \qquad (3.8)$$

where x_i and x_j are two points in the high-dimensional space and p_i represents the distance from each ith data point to its nearest neighbor. It gives a locally adaptive exponential kernel for each data point. Moreover, UMAP uses Eq. (3.9) for symmetrization of the high-dimensional probability:

$$p_{ij} = p_{i|j} + p_{j|i} - p_{i|j}p_{j|i}. \qquad (3.9)$$

UMAP defines the number of nearest neighbors of k as follows:

$$k_j = 2^{\sum_i p_{ij}}.$$

In optimizing the low-dimensional embedding we can again take some shortcuts. We can use stochastic gradient descent for the optimization process. To make the gradient descent problem easier it is beneficial if the

---

[6] Kullback–Leibler divergence ($D_{kl} = P||Q$) is a measure of how one probability distribution Q is different from a second, reference probability distribution P [109].

[7] Riemannian geometry is a form of differential non-Euclidean geometry developed by Bernhard Riemann, used to describe curved space [112].

final objective function is differentiable. We can arrange for that by using a smooth approximation of the actual membership strength function for the low-dimensional representation, selecting from a suitably versatile family. In practice, UMAP uses the family of curves of the form of Eq. (3.10):

$$\frac{1}{1 + ax^{2b}},\tag{3.10}$$

where $a \approx 1.93$ and $b \approx 0.79$ for default UMAP hyperparameters in our implementation. More details regarding the min-dist hyperparameter can be found in the appendix. Like all other advanced techniques which are presented in this book, both t-SNE and UMAP have their own advantages and disadvantages. Table 3.6 summarizes some of the characteristics of the mentioned dimensionality reduction and data visualization techniques.

Table 3.6 Details of utilized techniques for dimensionality reduction and data visualization.

Algorithm	Description	Characteristics
UMAP	Uses an exponential probability distribution in high dimensions but not necessarily Euclidean distances.	It does not apply normalization to either high- or low-dimensional probabilities. It often performs susceptibility to small data changes and parameter tuning difficulty [113].
t-SNE	Splits each high-dimensional object into a two- or three-dimensional point where all similar objects are modeled by nearby points.	It has the ability to preserve the local structures [109]. However, it has a slow performance due to nearest neighbor search queries and tends to get stuck in local optima [114].

References

[1] G. Miner, J. Elder, T. Hill, R. Nisbet, D. Delen, A. Fast, Practical Text Mining and Statistical Analysis for Non-Structured Text Data Applications, ITPro Collection, Elsevier Science, 2012.

[2] C. Roberts, Text Analysis for the Social Sciences: Methods for Drawing Statistical Inferences From Texts and Transcripts, Routledge Communication Series, Taylor & Francis, 1997.

[3] K. Krippendorff, Content Analysis: An Introduction to Its Methodology, Commtext Series, SAGE Publications, 1980.

[4] C. Adetuyi, O. Fidelis, Key concepts in transformational generative grammar, International Journal of English Language and Linguistics 1 (7) (2015) 1–9.

[5] C. Lovett, Warren Weaver, Scientist, Humanitarian, Carrollian: With a Bibliography of the Lewis Carroll Publications of Warren Weaver, Harry Ransom Humanities Research Center, 2000.

[6] W. Weaver, Translation, in: W.N. Locke, A.D. Boothe (Eds.), Machine Translation of Languages, MIT Press, Cambridge, MA, 1949, pp. 15–23, Reprinted from a memorandum written by Weaver in 1949.

[7] P. Seuren, Western Linguistics: A Historical Introduction, Wiley, 1998.

[8] K. Mahesh, S. Nirenburg, A situated ontology for practical NLP, in: Proceedings of the Workshop on Basic Ontological Issues in Knowledge Sharing, International Joint Conference on Artificial Intelligence (IJCAI-95), 1995.

[9] M. Womack, Symbols and Meaning: A Concise Introduction, Altamira Press, 2005.

[10] E. Charniak, Passing markers: A theory of contextual influence in language comprehension, Cognitive Science 7 (3) (1983) 171–190.

[11] C. Martin, C. Riesbeck, Uniform parsing and inferencing for learning, in: Proceedings of the Fifth AAAI National Conference on Artificial Intelligence, AAAI'86, AAAI Press, 1986, pp. 257–261.

[12] E. Ilkou, M. Koutraki, Symbolic vs sub-symbolic AI methods: Friends or enemies?, in: Proceedings of the CIKM 2020 Workshops Co-located with 29th ACM International Conference on Information and Knowledge Management (CIKM 2020), in: CEUR Workshop Proceedings, 2020.

[13] E. Ntoutsi, P. Fafalios, U. Gadiraju, V. Iosifidis, W. Nejdl, M. Vidal, S. Ruggieri, F. Turini, S. Papadopoulos, E. Krasanakis, I. Kompatsiaris, K. Kinder, C. Wagner, F. Karimi, M. Fernandez, H. Alani, B. Berendt, T. Kruegel, C. Heinze, S. Staab, Bias in data-driven artificial intelligence systems—an introductory survey, WIREs Data Mining and Knowledge Discovery 10 (3) (2020).

[14] M. Chitrao, R. Grishman, Statistical parsing of messages, in: Proceedings of the DARPA Speech and Natural Language, Workshop, Somerset, PA, June 24–27, 1990, Morgan Kaufmann, 1990.

[15] C. Manning, H. Schutze, Foundations of Statistical Natural Language Processing, MIT Press, 1999.

[16] E. Liddy, Natural language processing, in: Encyclopedia of Library and Information Science, 2nd edition, 2001.

[17] S. Paul, M. Agrawal, S. Rajput, S. Kumar, An information retrieval (IR) techniques for text mining on web for unstructured data, International Journal of Advanced Research in Computer Science and Software Engineering 4 (2) (2014) 67–70.

[18] S. Weiss, N. Indurkhya, T. Zhang, Information Retrieval and Text Mining, Springer, London, 2010, pp. 75–90.

[19] P. Sharma, R.K. Gupta, A novel web usage mining technique analyzing users behaviour using dynamic web log, International Journal of Computer Sciences and Engineering 5 (2017) 106–111.

[20] S. Kamruzzaman, F. Haider, A. Ryadh, Text classification using data mining, arXiv e-prints, arXiv:1009.4987, Sep. 2010.

[21] C. Aggarwal, C. Zhai, A Survey of Text Clustering Algorithms, Springer US, 2012, pp. 77–128.

[22] C. Manning, P. Raghavan, H. Schütze, Introduction to Information Retrieval, Cambridge University Press, 2008.

[23] S. Curiskis, B. Drake, T. Osborn, P. Kennedy, An evaluation of document clustering and topic modelling in two online social networks: Twitter and Reddit, Information Processing & Management 57 (April 2019).

[24] S. Fu, D. Chen, H. He, S. Liu, S. Moon, K.J. Peterson, F. Shen, L. Wang, Y. Wang, A. Wen, Y. Zhao, S. Sohn, H. Liu, Clinical concept extraction: A methodology review, Journal of Biomedical Informatics 109 (2020) 103526.

[25] S. Tulkens, S. Suster, W. Daelemans, Unsupervised concept extraction from clinical text through semantic composition, Journal of Biomedical Informatics 91 (2019) 103120.

[26] F. Millstein, Natural Language Processing With Python: Natural Language Processing Using NLTK, Frank Millstein, 2020.

[27] J. Byamugisha, C. Keet, B. DeRenzi, Toward an NLG system for Bantu languages: first steps with Runyankore (demo), 2017, pp. 154–155.

[28] C. Shorten, T. Khoshgoftaar, B. Furht, Text data augmentation for deep learning, Journal of Big Data 8 (July 2021).

[29] M. Collins, T. Koo, Discriminative Reranking for Natural Language Parsing, Computational Linguistics 31 (1) (2005) 25–70.

[30] H. Banaee, M. Ahmed, A. Loutfi, A framework for automatic text generation of trends in physiological time series data, in: 2013 IEEE International Conference on Systems, Man, and Cybernetics, 2013, pp. 3876–3881.

[31] A. Ramos-Soto, A. Bugarin, S. Barro, J. Taboada, Linguistic descriptions for automatic generation of textual short-term weather forecasts on real prediction data, IEEE Transactions on Fuzzy Systems 23 (1) (2015) 44–57.

[32] E. Reiter, R. Dale, Building applied natural language generation systems, Natural Language Engineering 3 (1) (1997) 57–87.

[33] T. McEnery, A. Hardie, Corpus Linguistics: Method, Theory and Practice, Cambridge Textbooks in Linguistics, Cambridge University Press, 2011.

[34] V. Korde, Text classification and classifiers: a survey, International Journal of Artificial Intelligence & Applications 3 (2012) 85–99.

[35] H. Dejean, J.-L. Meunier, Structuring documents according to their table of contents, in: Proceedings of the 2005 ACM Symposium on Document Engineering, DocEng '05, Association for Computing Machinery, 2005, pp. 2–9.

[36] M. Biba, F. Xhafa, Learning Structure and Schemas from Documents, Studies in Computational Intelligence, Springer, Berlin, Heidelberg, 2011.

[37] E.M. Nebot, Corpus-based activities in legal translator training, The Interpreter and Translator Trainer 2 (2) (2008) 221–252.

[38] M. Singh, A. Bhasin Surender, Using meta-heuristic approaches in web document clustering in web search, International Journal of Pure and Applied Mathematics 119 (2021) 2853–2861.

[39] Z. Wang, H. Zhang, A. Sarkar, A python-based interface for wide coverage lexicalized tree-adjoining grammars, The Prague Bulletin of Mathematical Linguistics 103 (2015) 139–159.

[40] A. Gatt, E. Reiter, SimpleNLG: A realisation engine for practical applications, in: Proceedings of the 12th European Workshop on Natural Language Generation, ENLG 2009, 2009, pp. 90–93.

[41] M. Rayner, P. Bouillon, N. Chatzichrisafis, M. Santaholma, M. Starlander, B. Hockey, Y. Nakao, H. Isahara, K. Kanzaki, MedSLT: a limited-domain unidirectional grammar-based medical speech translator, January 2006.

[42] M. Santaholma, in: Proceedings of the 16th Nordic Conference of Computational Linguistics (NODALIDA 2007), University of Tartu, Estonia, 2007, pp. 253–260.

[43] V. Garousi, S. Bauer, M. Felderer, NLP-assisted software testing: A systematic mapping of the literature, Information and Software Technology (2020) 106321.

[44] G. Carvalho, D. Falcao, F. Barros, A. Sampaio, A. Mota, L. Motta, M. Blackburn, Nat2testscr: Test case generation from natural language requirements based on SCR specifications, Science of Computer Programming 95 (2014) 275–297, Special Section: ACM SAC-SVT 2013 + Bytecode 2013.

[45] R. Mooney, R. Bunescu, Mining knowledge from text using information extraction, ACM SIGKDD Explorations Newsletter 7 (1) (2005) 3–10.

[46] R. Mooney, U. Nahm, Text mining with information extraction, in: W. Daelemans, T. du Plessis, C. Snyman, L. Teck (Eds.), Multilingualism and Electronic Language Management: Proceedings of the 4th International MIDP Colloquium, Van Schaik, South Africa, 2003, pp. 141–160.

[47] J. Deshmukh, M. Annervaz, S. Sengupta, A sequence modeling approach for structured data extraction from unstructured text, in: Proceedings of the 5th Workshop on Semantic Deep Learning (SemDeep-5), Association for Computational Linguistics, Macau, China, 2019, pp. 57–66.

[48] G. Bideault, L. Mioulet, C. Chatelain, T. Paquet, Using BLSTM for spotting regular expressions in handwritten documents, in: A. Fred, M. De Marsico, M. Figueiredo (Eds.), Pattern Recognition: Applications and Methods, Springer International Publishing, Cham, 2015, pp. 143–157.

[49] M. Califf, R. Mooney, Relational learning of pattern-match rules for information extraction, in: AAAI '99/IAAI '99, American Association for Artificial Intelligence, 1999, pp. 328–334.

[50] R. Lima, B. Espinasse, F. Freitas, An adaptive information extraction system based on wrapper induction with POS tagging, in: Proceedings of the 2010 ACM Symposium on Applied Computing, SAC '10, Association for Computing Machinery, 2010, pp. 1815–1820.

[51] B. Bengfort, R. Bilbro, T. Ojeda, Applied Text Analysis with Python: Enabling Language-Aware Data Products with Machine Learning, 1st edition, O'Reilly Media, Inc., 2018.

[52] F. Gomes, A. Ahmad, O. Leifler, K. Sandahl, E. Enoiu, Improving continuous integration with similarity-based test case selection, in: 2018 IEEE/ACM 13th International Workshop on Automation of Software Test (AST), 2018, pp. 39–45.

[53] F. Gomes, R. Torkar, P. Machado, Full modification coverage through automatic similarity-based test case selection, Information and Software Technology 80 (C) (2016) 124–137.

[54] R. Feldt, R. Torkar, T. Gorschek, W. Afzal, Searching for cognitively diverse tests: Towards universal test diversity metrics, in: 2008 IEEE International Conference on Software Testing Verification and Validation Workshop, 2008, pp. 178–186.

[55] T. Noor, H. Hemmati, A similarity-based approach for test case prioritization using historical failure data, in: 2015 IEEE 26th International Symposium on Software Reliability Engineering, 2015, pp. 58–68.

[56] Y. Ledru, A. Petrenko, S. Boroday, N. Mandran, Prioritizing test cases with string distances, Automated Software Engineering 19 (1) (2012) 65–95.

[57] A. Coutinho, E. Cartaxo, P. Machado, Analysis of distance functions for similarity-based test suite reduction in the context of model-based testing, Software Quality Journal 24 (2016) 407–445.

[58] G. Navarro, A guided tour to approximate string matching, ACM Computing Surveys 33 (1) (2001) 31–88.

[59] V. Levenshtein, Binary codes capable of correcting deletions, insertions, and reversals, Soviet Physics. Doklady 10 (1966) 707–710.

[60] M. Norouzi, D. Fleet, R. Salakhutdinov, Hamming distance metric learning, in: Advances in Neural Information Processing Systems, vol. 25, Curran Associates, Inc., 2012, pp. 1061–1069.

[61] B. Miranda, E. Cruciani, R. Verdecchia, A. Bertolino, FAST approaches to scalable similarity-based test case prioritization, in: Proceedings of the 40th International Conference on Software Engineering, ICSE '18, ACM, 2018, pp. 222–232.

[62] C. Bennett, P. Gacs, M. Li, P. Vitanyi, W. Zurek, Information distance, IEEE Transactions on Information Theory 44 (4) (1998) 1407–1423.

[63] P. Vitanyi, F. Balbach, R. Cilibrasi, M. Li, Normalized information distance, Information Theory and Statistical Learning (2009) 45–82.

[64] R. Cilibrasi, P. Vitanyi, Clustering by compression, IEEE Transactions on Information Theory 51 (4) (2005) 1523–1545.

[65] R. Feldt, S. Poulding, D. Clark, S. Yoo, Test set diameter: Quantifying the diversity of sets of test cases, in: 2016 IEEE International Conference on Software Testing, Verification and Validation, 2016, pp. 223–233.

[66] C. Henard, M. Papadakis, M. Harman, Y. Jia, Y. Le Traon, Comparing white-box and black-box test prioritization, in: 2016 IEEE/ACM 38th International Conference on Software Engineering, 2016, pp. 523–534.

[67] J. Kivijarvi, T. Ojala, T. Kaukoranta, A. Kuba, L. Nyul, O. Nevalainen, A comparison of lossless compression methods for medical images, Computerized Medical Imaging and Graphics 22 (4) (1998) 323–339.

[68] I. Numanagic, J. Bonfield, F. Hach, J. Voges, J. Ostermann, C. Alberti, M. Mattavelli, S.C. Sahinalp, Comparison of high-throughput sequencing data compression tools, Nature Methods 13 (12) (2016) 1005.

[69] J. Magnus, H. Neudecker, Matrix Differential Calculus with Applications in Statistics and Econometrics, John Wiley & Sons, 2019.

[70] J. Magnus, H. Neudecker, The commutation matrix: Some properties and applications, The Annals of Statistics 7 (2) (1979) 381–394.

[71] A. Kumari, M. Shashi, Vectorization of text documents for identifying unifiable news articles, International Journal of Advanced Computer Science and Applications 10 (2019) 305.

[72] S. Qaiser, R. Ali, Text mining: Use of TF-IDF to examine the relevance of words to documents, International Journal of Computer Applications 181 (1) (2018) 25–29.

[73] A. Huang, Similarity measures for text document clustering, in: Proceedings of the 6th New Zealand Computer Science Research Student Conference, 2008, pp. 49–56.

[74] E. Mueller, Commonsense reasoning using unstructured information, Chapter 18, in: Commonsense Reasoning, second edition, Morgan Kaufmann, 2015, pp. 315–335.

[75] K. Papineni, Why inverse document frequency?, in: Second Meeting of the North American Chapter of the Association for Computational Linguistics, 2001.

[76] H. Christian, M. Agus, D. Suhartono, Single document automatic text summarization using term frequency-inverse document frequency (TF-IDF), ComTech 7 (2016) 285–294.

[77] Y. Zhao, Y. Cen, Data Mining Applications with R, Elsevier Science, 2013.

[78] A. Aizawa, An information-theoretic perspective of TF–IDF measures, Information Processing and Management 39 (1) (2003) 45–65.

[79] Y. Zhang, R. Jin, Z. Zhou, Understanding bag-of-words model: a statistical framework, International Journal of Machine Learning and Cybernetics 1 (2010) 43–52.

[80] J. Brownlee, Deep Learning for Natural Language Processing: Develop Deep Learning Models for your Natural Language Problems, Machine Learning Mastery, 2017.

[81] T. Mikolov, K. Chen, G. Corrado, J. Dean, Efficient estimation of word representations in vector space, in: Proceedings of Workshop at ICLR 2013, January 2013.

[82] N. Witt, C. Seifert, Understanding the influence of hyperparameters on text embeddings for text classification tasks, in: J. Kamps, G. Tsakonas, Y. Manolopoulos, L. Iliadis, I. Karydis (Eds.), Research and Advanced Technology for Digital Libraries, Springer International Publishing, Cham, 2017, pp. 193–204.

[83] Q. Le, T. Mikolov, Distributed representations of sentences and documents, in: Proceedings of the 31st International Conference on International Conference on Machine Learning, ICML'14, vol. 32, JMLR, 2014, pp. II-1188–II-1196.

[84] A. Agresti, An Introduction to Categorical Data Analysis, Wiley Series in Probability and Statistics, Wiley, 2007.

[85] P. Rodriguez, M. Bautista, J. Gonzalez, S. Escalera, Beyond one-hot encoding: Lower dimensional target embedding, Image and Vision Computing 75 (2018) 21–31.

[86] M. Mahdavinejad, M. Rezvan, M. Barekatain, P. Adibi, P. Barnaghi, A. Sheth, Machine learning for internet of things data analysis: a survey, Digital Communications and Networks 4 (3) (2018) 161–175.

[87] P. Refaeilzadeh, L. Tang, H. Liu, Cross-Validation, Springer US, 2009, pp. 532–538.

[88] S. Russell, S. Russell, P. Norvig, Artificial Intelligence: A Modern Approach, Pearson Series in Artificial Intelligence, Pearson, 2020.

[89] P. Cunningham, M. Cord, S. Delany, Supervised Learning, Springer, Berlin, Heidelberg, 2008, pp. 21–49.

[90] E. Alpaydin, Machine Learning, revised and updated edition, The MIT Press Essential Knowledge Series, MIT Press, 2021.

[91] I. Witten, E. Frank, M. Hall, C. Pal, Data Mining: Practical Machine Learning Tools and Techniques, The Morgan Kaufmann Series in Data Management Systems, Elsevier Science, 2016.

[92] S. Kotsiantis, D. Kanellopoulos, P. Pintelas, Data preprocessing for supervised learning, International Journal of Computer Science 1 (2006) 111–117.

[93] M. Vijayarani, J. Ilamathi, M. Nithya, Preprocessing techniques for text mining – an overview, International Journal of Computer Science & Communication Networks (2015) 7–16.

[94] Y. Goldberg, G. Hirst, Neural Network Methods in Natural Language Processing, Synthesis Lectures on Human Language Technologies, Morgan & Claypool Publishers, 2017.

[95] J. Thanaki, Python Natural Language Processing, Packt Publishing, 2017.

[96] T. Mikolov, I. Sutskever, K. Chen, G. Corrado, J. Dean, Distributed representations of words and phrases and their compositionality, in: Proceedings of the 26th International Conference on Neural Information Processing Systems, vol. 2, NIPS'13, Curran Associates Inc., 2013, pp. 3111–3119.

[97] W. Meng, Y. Liu, Y. Huang, S. Zhang, F. Zaiter, B. Chen, D. Pei, A semantic-aware representation framework for online log analysis, in: 2020 29th International Conference on Computer Communications and Networks (ICCCN), IEEE, 2020, pp. 1–7.

[98] U. Alon, M. Zilberstein, O. Levy, E. Yahav, Code2Vec: Learning distributed representations of code, Proceedings of the ACM on Programming Languages 3 (2019) 40:1–40:29.

[99] S. Tahvili, L. Hatvani, E. Ramentol, R. Pimentel, W. Afzal, F. Herrera, A novel methodology to classify test cases using natural language processing and imbalanced learning, Engineering Applications of Artificial Intelligence 95 (2020) 1–13.

[100] Z. Wanwan, M. Jin, The effects of class imbalance and training data size on classifier learning: An empirical study, SN Computer Science 1 (February 2020).

[101] P. Cao, D. Zhao, O. Zaiane, Hybrid probabilistic sampling with random subspace for imbalanced data learning, Intelligent Data Analysis 18 (2014) 1089–1108.

[102] B. Liu, G. Tsoumakas, Dealing with class imbalance in classifier chains via random undersampling, Knowledge-Based Systems 192 (2020) 105292.

[103] A. Moreo, A. Esuli, F. Sebastiani, Distributional random oversampling for imbalanced text classification, in: Proceedings of the 39th International ACM SIGIR Conference on Research and Development in Information Retrieval, SIGIR '16, Association for Computing Machinery, 2016, pp. 805–808.

[104] N. Chawla, K. Bowyer, L. Hall, W. Kegelmeyer, Smote: Synthetic minority oversampling technique, Journal of Artificial Intelligence Research 16 (2002) 321–357.

[105] N. Naveen, Bayesian model selection for high-dimensional data, Chapter 4, in: Principles and Methods for Data Science, in: Handbook of Statistics, vol. 43, Elsevier, 2020, pp. 207–248.

[106] M. Blum, M. Nunes, D. Prangle, S. Sisson, A comparative review of dimension reduction methods in approximate Bayesian computation, Statistical Science 28 (2) (2013) 189–208.

[107] L. Van Der Maaten, E. Postma, J. Van den Herik, Dimensionality reduction: a comparative review, Journal of Machine Learning Research 10 (2009) 66–71.

[108] S. Kaski, J. Peltonen, Dimensionality reduction for data visualization [applications corner], IEEE Signal Processing Magazine 28 (2) (2011) 100–104.

[109] L. van der Maaten, G. Hinton, Visualizing data using t-SNE, Journal of Machine Learning Research 9 (2008) 2579–2605.

[110] Y. Kim, D. Kim, A. Kumar, R. Sarikaya, Efficient large-scale neural domain classification with personalized attention, in: Proceedings of the 56th Annual Meeting of the Association for Computational Linguistics (Volume 1: Long Papers), 2018, pp. 2214–2224.

[111] L. McInnes, J. Healy, N. Saul, L. Grossberger, UMAP: Uniform manifold approximation and projection, Journal of Open Source Software 3 (2018) 861.

[112] L. McInnes, J. Healy, J. Melville, UMAP: Uniform manifold approximation and projection for dimension reduction, arXiv preprint, arXiv:1802.03426, 2018.

[113] M. Espadoto, N.S.T. Hirata, A. Telea, Deep learning multidimensional projections, Information Visualization 19 (3) (2020) 247–269.

[114] L. van der Maaten, Fast optimization for t-SNE, in: NIPS Workshop on Challenges in Data Visualization, 2010.

CHAPTER FOUR

Decision intelligence and test optimization

Chapter points

- This chapter offers a comprehensive introduction to decision intelligence and decision support systems and describes how they can be employed for test optimization purposes in the industry.
- An overview of decision-making in volatility, uncertainty, complexity, and ambiguity conditions and situations is presented.
- The different aspects of test optimization are discussed.

"True optimization is the revolutionary contribution of modern research to decision processes."

George Dantzig

4.1. The evolution of artificial intelligence

Artificial intelligence in Greek antiquity was just a figment of the imagination in the minds of poets such as Hesiod and Homer [1]. However, today artificial intelligence is taking root in different aspects of our daily lives such as weather forecasts, email spam filtering, and auto-correct functions. Although artificial intelligence is not a new concept, it took almost a century for artificial intelligence to become a plausible reality from fiction [2]. Due to the growth of mobile and cloud platforms, artificial intelligence plays a vital role in the technological revolution. Therefore, artificial intelligence is considered to be the driver of the "Second Information Revolution" or the "Fourth Industrial Revolution". Like all other journeys of a thousand miles which began with a single step, artificial intelligence has also had its journey, a cut of which is shown in Fig. 4.1.

The First Industrial Revolution (also known as Industry 1.0) began in the 18th century, when the agricultural societies became more industrialized [3]. The steam-based machines, the transcontinental railroad, and electricity, which permanently changed society, were invented during Industry 1.0. Although Industry 1.0 had a big impact on society, no period introduced more changes than the Second Industrial Revolution (from the

Artificial Intelligence Methods for Optimization of the Software Testing Process
https://doi.org/10.1016/B978-0-32-391913-5.00015-4

late 19th to the early 20th century) [4]. Electrification can be considered as the final major development (e.g., assembly line and mass production) during the Second Industrial Revolution, among all other advances [4,5]. The Third Industrial Revolution (also known as Industry 3.0 or the Digital Revolution) began in the latter half of the 20th century. During Industry 3.0, we observed a big transition from mechanical electronic technology to digital computers [6]. This shift has led to another revolution in information technology.

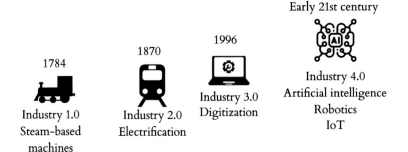

Figure 4.1 A cut of the evolution of artificial intelligence (the Fourth Industrial Revolution). Source: Authors' own contribution.

Gerald Brock[1] in his book regarding the Information Revolution emphasizes that information technology has dramatically changed our daily life twice in history [8]:

"the use of telegraphs and telephones for integrating national markets during the first information revolution and the use of computer-enhanced communications in the second information revolution."

Considering the continuous development in information technology in the digitization era, the industry has faced its Fourth Revolution known as Industry 4.0 in the early 21st century (see Fig. 4.1). The Fourth Industrial Revolution mainly involves advances in artificial intelligence, the Internet of Things, and robotics [9]. Like the previous revolutions, Industry 4.0 has improved the quality of our daily life. Moreover, employing artificial intelligence in large industries helps us to predict risks, optimize operations, process large-scale structured and unstructured data, and also visualize data in a consumable way [10].

---

[1] Gerald W. Brock is Professor of Telecommunication and Director of the Graduate Telecommunication Program at George Washington University, and was previously Common Carrier Bureau Chief at the Federal Communications Commission [7].

However, the main idea of artificial intelligence is mimicking human intelligence processes by computer systems, making decisions in different environments, in critical situations, and in different conditions [11]. In the rest of this chapter, we briefly describe why artificial intelligence is important in decision-making processes.

4.2. Decision-making in a VUCA world

As hinted before, rapid technological changes in the recent decades are impacting different areas of our daily life, e.g., culture, engineering, and the economy. This technology acceleration can be challenging if the learning process does not match the expectations [12], or if the rate of changes is outpacing our ability to adapt. Paying no attention to the rapid technological changes and following the old ways of decision-making might drag us into a challenging decision-making environment called the volatility, uncertainty, complexity, and ambiguity (VUCA) world.

Table 4.1 VUCA, opposites, and examples.

Acronym	Definition	Opposite	Example
V	Volatility	Stability	Facing rapid changes
U	Uncertainty	Predictability	Feeling unclear about the present and future
C	Complexity	Linearity	Experiencing chaos due to different factors
A	Ambiguity	Explicitness	Feeling less aware and clear than usual

The acronym VUCA stands for **V**olatility, **U**ncertainty, **C**omplexity, and **A**mbiguity, which in today's technology can be positive as well as negative. The VUCA world concept was for the first time proposed by Bennis[2] and Nanus[3] in 1987 drawing on leadership theories. In order to get a clearer understanding of the VUCA dimensions, we contrast them with their opposites and provide examples in Table 4.1.

Most of the currently existing technologies are limited to solving only a subset of the decision-making challenges, especially in the VUCA environment. Therefore, decision support systems, business intelligence, and

---

[2] Warren Gamaliel Bennis (1925–2014) was an American University Professor and author, widely regarded as a pioneer of the contemporary field of leadership studies.

[3] Burt Nanus is an American Professor at the University of Southern California.

decision intelligence have become a critical part of the technology development in the industry.

There are several models for performing a decision-making process, e.g., iterative decision-making, rational and non-rational decision-making.[4] Fig. 4.2 depicts a custom version of an iterative decision-making process.

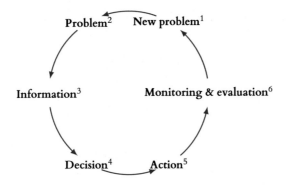

Figure 4.2 A custom version of an iterative decision-making process.

Generally, an iterative decision-making process involves the following steps:

- As the first step, we need to gather all the required information. This step can be performed in several meetings with the team members to ask for contributions, where the team members can explain their experiences with the same problem. The goal for this step is to shift an unknown problem to a real problem (for the problem, see step 2 in Fig. 4.2). This transaction can help us define what exactly needs to be solved.
- Step 3 can be performed by conducting several brainstorming sessions. A draft of the possible solutions to the defined problem can be reviewed at this stage. One of the universal keys in iterative decision-making processes is creativity. Solving some of the real industrial problems requires out-of-the-box thinking. For analyzing all the proposed solutions in this step the following parameters need to be considered:
  - *Feasibility.*
  - *Which solution can be implemented quickly?*
  - *Cost-effectiveness.*

---

[4] The term "non-rational" denotes a heterogeneous class of theories of decision-making designed to overcome problems with traditional "rational" theories.

- *Time, deadline, and required effort.*
- By observing all the outlined parameters, we can make a decision towards solving the problem (see step 4 in Fig. 4.2). It might be the case that more than one solution has been selected which could satisfy our pre-defined parameters. However, if the time and budget allow, more than one solution can be a candidate for implementation. Moreover, when it comes to reaching a decision, the following points need to be considered:
  - **Objective.** We need to determine the objective. What problems and issues stand in the way of reaching this objective, and how can we overcome these problems?
  - **Resources.** What can we utilize that will help us reach the decision? Whether it is financial or human capital, knowing which resources are at our disposal can make the decision-making process a lot smoother.
  - **Alternatives.** A singular approach to reaching the objective might not be sufficient. Backups, contingencies, and alternatives are therefore a crucial part of decision-making. However we carry it out, a thorough analysis of each possible decision's outcome will ensure we have alternative routes to explore if things do not properly work out.
  - **Leadership.** Once we have reached a decision, having the confidence to act on our plans is key. As well as our own leadership, we should be aware of the leadership skills of others within the company. Including them in the decision-making process could improve our chances of success and make things go a lot more smoothly as a result.
- Step 5 is mainly about the action which indicates the selected candidate solution(s) is ready for execution.
- Monitoring and evaluation are always the final steps (see step 6 in Fig. 4.2) of an iterative decision-making process. Evaluating the obtained results can help the decision-maker learn lessons that will improve their decision-making abilities.

However, as stated before, most of the existing technologies can help us solve a subset of decision-making problems. We are still dependent on the subject matter experts in the industry, even when a human decision might take more time and does not provide higher accuracy. Combining the new and innovative technologies with academic disciplines and human interactions can help us improve our decisions and thereby the world around us. In this regard, decision intelligence has emerged as a new critical science that focuses on several aspects of selecting between different options. The basic idea is that decisions are based on our understanding of how actions lead to outcomes.

"...the key here is that in order for us to let the data drive the decision, that decision context has to be framed upfront. So the decision-maker has to understand what it actually takes to get them to want to do one thing versus another."

Cassie Kozyrkov, Chief Decision Scientist, Google, 2018

The intelligent decision is an autonomous cognitive-based approach for making a knowledgeable, in-depth analysis and concise decision about the systems [13]. The intelligent decision facilitates the decision-making process by employing previous knowledge, insights, and also the taken decision. Therefore, intelligent decisions can be considered as a solution for solving real industrial problems, especially in the VUCA world. In Fig. 4.3 we illustrate the main steps of an intelligent decision-making process that is designed based on the iterative decision-making process shown in Fig. 4.2.

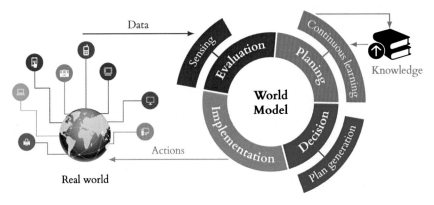

Figure 4.3 The steps of an intelligent decision-making process. Source: Authors' own contribution inspired by the proposed model by Fawkes [14].

As we can see in Fig. 4.3, most of the presented steps in an iterative decision-making process are employed in an intelligent decision-making process. However, one of the main differences between an intelligent decision process and an iterative decision-making process is the continuous learning process from a stream of data (see Fig. 4.3).

Definition 4.1. Continual Learning is the ability to learn adaptively and continually from the external world (stream of data). Continual learning enables the autonomous incremental development of ever more complex skills and knowledge [15], [16].

As stated earlier, the main goal of employing artificial intelligence in the industry is to deploy models through a new production environment. In this regard, continuous learning supports the ability of a model to autonomously learn and adapt in production as new data comes continuously. In fact, the old models of the iterative and rational decision-making processes use static learning, which means they will learn once and deploy once. However, in an intelligent decision-making process, an adaptive learning process is embedded, which will learn and also deploy continuously.

Furthermore, as we can see in Fig. 4.3, the opportunity of having more than one decision is considered, where several plans can be generated during the decision-making process. Another advantage of having an intelligent decision-making process is the way that we gather the data and evaluate the performance of the model. As shown in Fig. 4.3, the data will be captured from several sources and the action of the decision will be analyzed continuously as well. Later in this book, we are going to exemplify how the presented model in Fig. 4.3 can be utilized for solving industrial problems for different test optimization purposes.

4.3. Multi-criterion intelligent test optimization methodology

Besides solving the VUCA environment in the decision-making process, most real industrial or even life decision-making problems have several conflicting criteria and objectives to be considered simultaneously [17]. For solving those kinds of problems, we need to utilize a methodology that can handle multi-criteria choices among alternatives [18].

Definition 4.2. Multi-criterion decision-making is a branch of operations research that involves imprecision and vagueness which explicitly evaluates multiple conflicting criteria in decision-making simultaneously [19], [20].

The main advantage of employing a multi-criterion decision-making methodology is the ability to break down the decision problem into smaller pieces while considering that the value of each part is important. This advantage can help the decision-makers to (1) have a better overview of the initial problem, (2) analyze each part separately, and thereby (3) provide a meaningful solution for the initial problem. In this regard, multi-criterion decision-making can be effectively handled by fuzzy sets[5] and also fuzzy decision-making[6] techniques [19]. To get a better understanding of a multi-criterion decision-making solution, we exemplified the required steps by providing an industrial use case in Fig. 4.4.

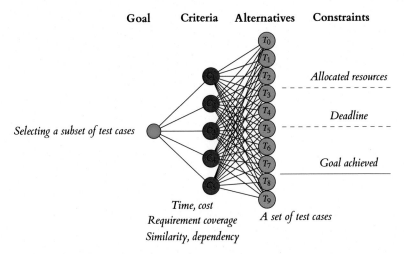

Figure 4.4 An illustration of a multi-criterion decision-making problem with several criteria, different alternatives, and constraints. Source: Tahvili et al. [23].

Generally, a multi-criterion decision-making solution includes the following components:

1. **Goal.** What is the main goal of this decision-making problem? For instance, we have a large set of test cases and we need to select a subset of them for execution.

2. **Criteria.** Which parameters should be considered and satisfied in this decision-making problem? The list of important criteria can be provided by the subject matter experts in the industry. For instance, for the mentioned problem in Fig. 4.4, we have to identify the *test cases' execution time, their requirement coverage, the cost of each test execution, and the similarity between test cases* as the most critical criteria for test case selection. As we can see in Fig. 4.4, our five different criteria (C_1 to C_5) have a direct effect on every single alternative (test cases).

---

[5] A fuzzy set is characterized by a membership function which maps the members of the universe into the unit interval, thus assigning to elements of the universe degrees of belongingness concerning a set [21].

[6] Fuzzy decision-making is a collection of single- or multi-criterion techniques aiming at selecting the best alternative case of imprecise, incomplete, and vague data [22].

3. **Decision alternatives.** What alternatives do we have in the decision-making process? In this case, the test cases are our alternatives, where a subset of them needs to be selected and ranked for the test execution.

4. **Evaluation of the impact of each criterion on each alternative.** For performing this step, usually compensatory aggregation[7] methods such as the analytic hierarchy process [26] and the technique for order of preference by similarity to ideal solution [27] are recommended to be utilized.

5. **The problem's constraints and limitations.** Besides considering the impact of the critical criteria on the decision alternatives, we also need to monitor the limitation and the constraints. For instance, as illustrated in Fig. 4.4 we might have allocated resources for executing just three test cases. Or after executing five test cases, we face a deadline. "Goal Achieved" in Fig. 4.4 indicates that testers detect the expected number of faults after executing eight test cases in this particular order. The last two test cases (T_8, T_9) are thus considered redundant. Therefore, it is very important to consider the limitations in advance.

4.4. Static and continuous test optimization process

Based on the highlighted factors in this chapter, now it is clear that artificial intelligence is making its presence known more and more across a broad range of industries. Some studies show that employing artificial intelligence technologies in software engineering is already revolutionizing the way that developers work. Artificial intelligence is heavily involved in many aspects of software engineering, from project planning and testing to user experience and quality assurance. In summary, artificial intelligence has resulted in significant increases in productivity, quality, and speed [28], [29], which are the main goals of all optimization processes in the industry. The test optimization process can lead to using the testing resources in a more efficient way without compromising the test accuracy or test coverage [25]. In an efficient test optimization process, we can minimize the risk of unnecessary failure, eliminate unnecessary manual steps, automate some test steps, reduce errors, and avoid duplicate work [28]. The process of software test optimization can be performed statically or continuously [30].

---

[7] In a compensatory aggregation method, a set of alternatives and criteria need to be defined and identified, respectively. The compensatory methods measure weight for each criterion and also calculate the geometric distance between each alternative [24], [25].

Test optimization can be divided into two main sub-disciplines, static and continuous optimization, where they can be employed separately or together. A static optimization approach generally can be utilized on a pre-defined testing process, where the testing artifacts, e.g., requirement, test cases, and test scripts, are already created and we just need to optimize the testing process once. Static optimization is an appropriate approach for instance for regression or unit testing, where subsamples of test cases are going to be executed or we are dealing with rather simple test cases. However, continuous optimization of a testing process requires significant added effort in terms of designing and implementing the solution without stopping the testing process. More complex test cases or test levels (e.g., integration testing) can be considered for continuous optimization.

In fact, the main difference between static and continuous optimization in a testing process is the considered time for optimization. In a large industry, monitoring the efficiency of the investment (e.g., the required effort for optimization and the returned benefit) in all optimization processes can guide the stakeholders to select a proper optimization approach. Although the new artificial intelligence technologies show promising results, it might be hard to implement due to the required costs and effort. In this regard, during the optimization process (especially continuous optimization) we need to dynamically evaluate the performance, gains, and the reduction in time requirements.

In Fig. 4.5 we illustrate an overall overview of a continuous optimization process in a testing process. The interconnected items shown in Fig. 4.5 yield the following four main stages for applying artificial intelligence in continuous test optimization:

1. **Planning.** Artificial intelligence methods can be applied to different aspects of the test planning, e.g., measuring what test coverage is required, analyzing the similarity of the requirements, and also identifying the inadequate tests coordinated with the database or database-driven tool. Employing artificial intelligence in the planning step can significantly minimize the manual work required to design and analyze the requirements and test cases while simultaneously increasing the quality of the test artifacts. Moreover, to train the artificial intelligence models, the data-gathering process should be performed continuously. The required data for applying an artificial intelligence-based solution can be captured from various sources, e.g., the test environments and the test artifacts (requirements specification, test cases, and test results). As we can see in Fig. 4.5, there is a direct connection between the optimiza-

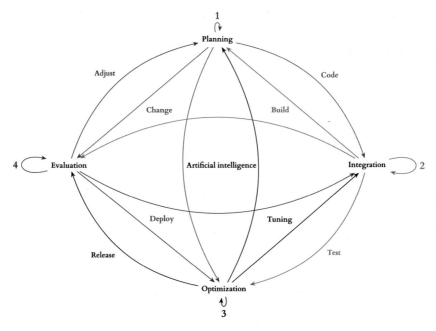

Figure 4.5 A continuous test optimization process using artificial intelligence. Source: Authors' own contribution.

tion and planning stages, which indicates that the initial test plan needs to be modified based on the results. As mentioned before, test planning and test design are two critical activities that are directly dependent on the testing teams' skills. Creating the test cases automatically based on the requirements in terms of test automation is another advantage of using artificial intelligence technologies in this step.

2. **Integration.** This stage focuses more on the test execution, where it can consist of various levels of testing from unit to acceptance testing. Regardless of the testing procedure (manual, semi-automated, or fully automated), the test results need to flow back for further analysis and decision-making. Selecting a subset of test cases for execution, dynamically scheduling test cases for execution based on the execution results, and merging/removing some of the test cases can be considered as potential artificial intelligence use cases. Moreover, analyzing a large set of the created data by algorithms after each execution can help the testing team overcome the problems of noise, the introduction of a new feature, and various other changes. On the other hand, employing an artificial intelligence-based solution on the failed test cases can reduce

the troubleshooting and debugging time. Furthermore, the high-risk areas in the source code repository can be identified faster by applying artificial intelligence at the integration stage.

3. **Optimization.** The artificial intelligence model also needs to be trained during continuous testing optimization, where the generated data from the previous stages can be used. Furthermore, hyperparameter tuning,[8] which means choosing a set of optimal hyperparameters for a learning algorithm (see the *"Tuning"* arrow in Fig. 4.5), should be done in this stage. Hyperparameter tuning can help the testing team to improve the proficiency of the artificial intelligence models, where it can be performed via employing different approaches, e.g., grid search, random search, Bayesian optimization, and population-based approaches.

4. **Evaluation.** The proposed artificial intelligence-based solution needs to be evaluated concerning specific metrics (confusion matrix, return on investment, internal rate of return) in this stage.

However, in a continuous testing process, a large and new dataset might be generated, thus the optimization process should be directly connected to the *planning, integration, optimization,* and *evaluation* stages. The mentioned stages in Fig. 4.5 are exemplified with several industrial case studies later in this book. Considering all mentioned issues and limitations in large industries, test automation has a high demand for optimization purposes [31]. However, other artificial intelligence-based optimization approaches, which can be applied in several stages in Fig. 4.5, have recently received a great deal of attention. In the following, we provide some optimization approaches where we later combine them with the artificial intelligence models for continuously optimizing a testing process.

4.4.1 Test case selection

Test case selection can be considered a proper optimization approach, e.g., in exploratory and regression testing, where the behavior of a modified software program can be verified by selecting a subset of test cases for re-execution. Indeed, not all created test cases need to be executed at the same testing level as they can instead be tested at some other testing levels, for instance, acceptance testing, where all test cases have already been executed at least once and only a few test cases need to be selected for re-execution. Selecting and evaluating a subset of generated test cases for execution is a

---

[8] Also known as hyperparameter optimization.

technique to optimize a testing process [32]. Yoo and Harman [33] formulate test case selection as follows:

Definition 4.3 (Test case selection problem). ***Given:*** *The program, P, the modified version of P, P′, and a test suite, T.*
Problem: *To find a subset of T, T′, with which to test P′.*

In other scenarios where the testers are involved in minimum planning and maximum test execution such as exploratory testing, test case selection can be used for optimization purposes. Some methods of compensatory aggregation for selecting a subset of test cases for execution are presented by Tahvili in [25].

4.4.2 Test case prioritization

To increase the rate of fault detection, all generated test cases should be ranked for execution in such a way that test cases of higher importance are ranked higher. Test case prioritization can be applied almost at all testing levels with the main purpose of detecting faults earlier in the software product.

To increase the rate of fault detection, all generated test cases should be ranked for execution in such a way that more important test cases are ranked higher [34]. Test case prioritization can be applied at all testing levels with the main purpose of earlier fault detection in a product under test. The problem of test case prioritization is defined by Yoo and Harman [33] as follows.

Definition 4.4 (Test case prioritization problem). ***Given:*** *A test suite, T, the set of permutations of T, PT, and a function from PT to real numbers, f :* $PT \to \mathbb{R}$.
Problem: *To find a $T' \in PT$ that maximizes f.*

The main difference between Definition 4.3 and Definition 4.4 is the number of test cases, where a subset of test cases will be removed in test case selection. However, all generated test cases will be ranked for execution in test case prioritization. The problem of test prioritization is addressed later in this book via analyzing several industrial case studies.

4.4.3 Test suite minimization

Test suite minimization has the goal to identify and eliminate redundant test cases in order to reduce the number of test cases to run [33]. There are several approaches for test suite minimization. However, all of them aim to identify unique and effective test cases and remove other created test cases from a test suite. The definition of uniqueness differs from case to case and it should be matched with the allocated testing resources as well. The main advantage of applying test suite minimization is reducing the testing time and cost while maintaining quality.

Definition 4.5 (Test suite minimization problem). ***Given:*** *A test suite, T, and a set of requirements $Rq_1, \ldots, Rq_n$, that must be tested by a subset of T, $(T_1, \ldots, T_n)$, where each test case in T is associated with each of Rq_i, where any one of the test cases t_j belonging to T can be used to achieve requirement Rq_i.* ***Problem:*** *To find T' of test cases from T that satisfy all Rq_i.*

In order words, the end of a typical testing process is whenever all requirements in $Rq_1, \ldots, Rq_n$ are tested. As we can see in Definition 4.5, a requirement, Rq_i, is planned to be tested by any test case, t_j, that belongs to T_i, which is a subset of T. Therefore, the representative set of test cases is the hitting set of T_i. Furthermore, in order to maximize the effect of minimization, T' should be the minimal hitting set of T_i [35].

4.4.4 Random, exploratory, and parallel test execution

One of the key features for optimization a testing process is the way that the testing team executes test cases. Resource efficiency in the testing domain can be defined as splitting test cases properly between testers, test channels, and test stations. In this regard, several approaches such as risk-based, rapid, and parallel testing can be applied where the critical and error-prone parts of the software need to be tested first and faster [36]. The following paragraphs provide definitions and some examples of random, exploratory, and parallel test execution.

Definition 4.6 (Random testing). Random testing is a kind of black box software testing technique where programs are tested by generating random and independent inputs. Results of the output are compared against software specifications to verify that the test is passed or failed [37].

Random testing is a useful approach whenever the testing team does not have enough time to write and execute several test cases. Moreover, random testing can also be applied for testing highly complex problems where it is impossible to test all combinations [37].

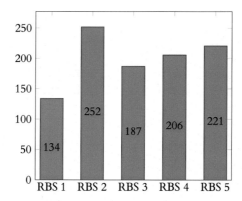

Figure 4.6 An overview of the serial test execution for testing five radio base stations (RBSs) at Ericsson AB. The *X*-axis represents the products (RBSs). The numbers inside the bars are the number of required test cases. Source: Landin et al. [40].

Definition 4.7 (Exploratory testing). Exploratory testing is an approach to software testing that is concisely described as simultaneous learning, test design, and test execution.

Exploratory testing is a valuable approach to uncover non-obvious errors, especially in test automation, where a large set of test scripts are scheduled for execution. However, since performing exploratory testing is expensive, the testing team needs to have a clear scope that focuses on a specific area of the software [38].

Definition 4.8 (Parallel test execution). Parallel testing or parallel test execution is a process of running the test case in parallel rather than one after the other. In parallel testing, the program's multiple parts (or modules) execute together, saving the testing team a lot of time and effort [39].

In other words, parallel testing means using multiple versions of a software application that are tested with the same input on different test stations simultaneously [39]. For instance, test cases can be executed on several test stations in parallel, which leads to a reduction in test execution time. In order to exemplify the concept of parallel test execution, we can review Fig. 4.6 and Fig. 4.7, which show serial and parallel test execution for testing the same products (radio base station [RBSs]) at Ericsson AB, respectively. As we can see in Fig. 4.6, five products (RBSs) are assigned to be tested on five different test stations. Although the number of required test cases for testing each RBS is different, there are some similarities between the designed test cases. In the presented serial testing approach in

Fig. 4.6, all created test cases for each RBS need to be tested separately, where one unique test station is assigned to each RBS and its test cases.

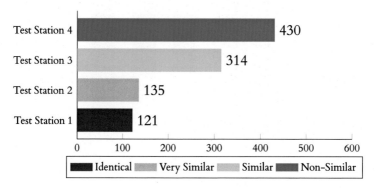

Figure 4.7 An overview of the parallel execution process for testing five radio base stations (RBSs) at Ericsson. The *X*-axis represents the required test cases and the *Y*-axis shows the number of the test stations. Source: Landin et al. [40].

In fact, even if two RBSs have several test cases in common (identical), then those identical test cases should be executed at least twice on two different test stations. However, employing artificial intelligence techniques such as natural language processing on the created test cases can help the test managers to schedule similar test cases on the same test station. So just to recap, if two test cases are similar, they might require the same test environment setup, or they have the same pre-condition, or they are designed to test the same function. Thus, applying parallel test execution for similar test cases can significantly decrease the testing time. Fig. 4.7 shows the proposed parallel test execution for the presented RBSs in Fig. 4.6, where the test cases are classified into four classes based on their similarities.

4.4.5 Intelligence test scheduling

Test scheduling is the practice of running tests automatically, managing test data, and utilizing results to improve software quality. It is primarily a quality assurance measure, but its activities involve the commitment of the entire software production team.

Most of the previous work [32,41–43] on test case selection and prioritization is applicable before test execution, which means that they do not monitor the test results after each execution. To optimize the testing process consciously, the execution of each test case needs to be recorded and analyzed. Selecting and prioritizing test cases for execution based on their execution results leads us to utilize the term of test case scheduling as a proper technique for addressing test optimization issues. Tahvili et al. [30] propose the following definition for the problem of test case scheduling.

Definition 4.9 (Test case scheduling problem). *Given: A test suite, T, where for all subsets of T, $A \subseteq T$, we have the set of all permutations of A, SPA; for all $B \subseteq T$, we have the set of all possible outputs after execution of the test cases in B, R; and for each $r \in R$, we have the function $f_r : SPA \to \mathbb{R}$.*
Problem: (1) To find a prioritized set of T, T', considering the function $f_\emptyset : PT \to \mathbb{R}$, where PT is the set of permutations of T, (2) to execute the test cases in T' until the first failure (if any), and (3) to update the previous procedure for $T - T_p$, considering the function f_{r_e}, until $T_p = T$, where T_p is the set of passed test cases and r_e is the output of the executed test cases.

Indeed, the executed test cases need to be saved in r_e and the prioritizing process should be continued until all generated test cases are executed at least one time.

We need to consider that the main difference between Definitions 4.3, 4.4, and 4.9 lies in monitoring the results of the test executions, which leads to a dynamic test optimization process. If no failures occur after the first execution, then we only need to prioritize test cases once, according to Definition 4.4.

4.4.6 Test automation

Test automation is a popular approach, especially in regression testing. Instead of regressing the same test cases each time, this process can be fully automated. Test automation can be a suitable test optimization approach in large industries where some of the features of the software hardly change when a new build is made [31]. However, the maintenance of test scripts needs to be considered as a recurring expense which is usually a low cost.

Even if artificial intelligence can be applied in different ways during system testing, we argue that a simpler taxonomy focusing on the generic steps in a system level testing process can help in the understanding of the points of applications during system level testing. Many artificial intelligence approaches are applied to more than one system testing step and the results can be combined.

The following steps where artificial intelligence is applied to system testing are outlined in Fig. 4.8:
- *Test planning and analysis.* Artificial intelligence can be applied in this activity by determining what is going to be tested and optimizing a test

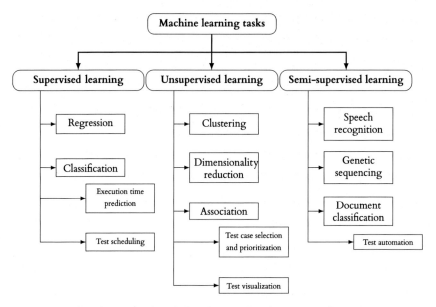

Figure 4.8 Machine learning tasks, sub-disciplines, and applications in software testing. Source: Authors' own contribution.

plan by analyzing the test artifacts created during software development (e.g., requirement documents, test specifications).

- *Test design.* Artificial intelligence can be applied in this activity for automating system level test design. This has been proposed to allow test cases to be created with less effort. The goal is to automatically find a small set of test cases that check the correctness of the system and guard against (previous as well as future) faults.
- *Test execution.* After test cases have been generated, artificial intelligence can be applied during the test selection and execution process. This can determine which test cases will be executed during regression testing, which system configurations will be evaluated by each test case, and which test setups are available for the actual running of each test case.
- *Test evaluation.* As the test cases are executed, valuable data is generated that artificial intelligence can exploit through data-mining techniques to evaluate the test results and localize suspicious program behavior as well as to cluster similar and independent faults.

Optimizing each of these test activities using artificial intelligence is a process we call test optimization which is outlined in more detail in this book. The overall architecture of a generic artificial intelligence-based system testing process used for test optimization is shown in Fig. 4.8. This approach starts with only two inputs: the choice of the representation of the problem based on the available raw data and the definition of the heuristic function. With these two, an engineer can implement artificial intelligence-based system testing using optimization algorithms and obtain results.

References

[1] A. Mayor, Gods and Robots: Myths, Machines, and Ancient Dreams of Technology, Princeton University Press, 2020.
[2] L. Steels, R. Brooks, The artificial life route to artificial intelligence: Building situated embodied agents, 1995.
[3] P. Deane, The First Industrial Revolution, Cambridge University Press, 1979.
[4] C. More, Understanding the Industrial Revolution, Routledge, 2000.
[5] V. Smil, Creating the Twentieth Century: Technical Innovations of 1867–1914 and Their Lasting Impact, Oxford University Press, 2005.
[6] J. Rifkin, The Third Industrial Revolution: How Lateral Power Is Transforming Energy, the Economy, and the World, St. Martin's Publishing Group, 2011.
[7] G. Brock, The Telecommunications Industry: The Dynamics of Market Structure, Harvard Economic Studies, Harvard University Press, 1981.
[8] G. Brock, The Second Information Revolution, Harvard University Press, 2003.
[9] K. Schwab, The Fourth Industrial Revolution, Penguin Books Limited, 2017.
[10] A. Torre-Bastida, J. Del Ser, N. Bilbao, M. Ilardia, S. Campos, I. Lana, Big data for transportation and mobility: Recent advances, trends and challenges, IET Intelligent Transport Systems 12 (July 2018).
[11] S. Dick, Artificial intelligence, Harvard Data Science Review 1 (1) (July 2019).
[12] S. Latha, P. Christopher, VUCA in engineering education: Enhancement of faculty competency for capacity building, in: 9th World Engineering Education Forum (WEEF 2019) Proceedings: Disruptive Engineering Education for Sustainable Development, Procedia Computer Science 172 (2020) 741–747.
[13] Z. Kowalczuk, M. Czubenko, An intelligent decision-making system for autonomous units based on the mind model, in: 2018 23rd International Conference on Methods Models in Automation Robotics (MMAR), 2018, pp. 1–6.
[14] A. Fawkes, Developments in artificial intelligence – opportunities and challenges for military modeling and simulation, 2017.
[15] J. Schwarz, W. Czarnecki, J. Luketina, A. Grabska-Barwinska, Y. Teh, R. Pascanu, R. Hadsell, Progress and amp; compress: A scalable framework for continual learning, in: Proceedings of the 35th International Conference on Machine Learning, in: Proceedings of Machine Learning Research, vol. 80, 2018, pp. 4528–4537.
[16] B. Liu, Learning on the job: Online lifelong and continual learning, Proceedings of the AAAI Conference on Artificial Intelligence 34 (2020) 13544–13549.
[17] A. Jahan, K.L. Edwards, M. Bahraminasab, 4. Multi-criteria decision-making for materials selection, in: A. Jahan, K. Edwards, M. Bahraminasab (Eds.), Multi-Criteria Decision Analysis for Supporting the Selection of Engineering Materials in Product Design, second edition, Butterworth-Heinemann, 2016, pp. 63–80.
[18] I. Ozsahin, D. Ozsahin, B. Uzun, M. Mustapha, Introduction, Chapter 1, in: Applications of Multi-Criteria Decision-Making Theories in Healthcare and Biomedical Engineering, Academic Press, 2021, pp. 1–2.
[19] B. Sarkar, 14. Fuzzy decision making and its applications in cotton fibre grading, in: A. Majumdar (Ed.), Soft Computing in Textile Engineering, in: Woodhead Publishing Series in Textiles, Woodhead Publishing, 2011, pp. 353–383.

[20] L. Rew, Acknowledging intuition in clinical decision making, Journal of Holistic Nursing 18 (2) (2000) 94–108.

[21] I. Vlachos, G. Sergiadis, Intuitionistic fuzzy image processing, in: Soft Computing in Image Processing: Recent Advances, Springer, Berlin, Heidelberg, 2007, pp. 383–414.

[22] C. Kahraman, S. Onar, B. Oztayşi, Fuzzy decision making: Its pioneers and supportive environment, in: Fuzzy Logic in Its 50th Year: New Developments, Directions and Challenges, Springer International Publishing, 2016, pp. 21–58.

[23] S. Tahvili, W. Afzal, M. Saadatmand, M. Bohlin, D. Sundmark, S. Larsson, Towards earlier fault detection by value-driven prioritization of test cases using fuzzy TOPSIS, in: 13th International Conference on Information Technology: New Generations (ITNG), 2016.

[24] S. Greco, A. Ishizaka, M. Tasiou, G. Torrisi, On the methodological framework of composite indices: A review of the issues of weighting, aggregation, and robustness, Social Indicators Research 141 (2019) 1–34.

[25] S. Tahvili, Multi-criteria optimization of system integration testing, PhD thesis, Malardalen University, 12 2018.

[26] T. Saaty, Decision-making with the AHP: Why is the principal eigenvector necessary, European Journal of Operational Research 145 (1) (2003) 85–91.

[27] M. Behzadian, S. Khanmohammadi, M. Yazdani, J. Ignatius, A state-of the-art survey of TOPSIS applications, Expert Systems with Applications 39 (17) (2012) 13051–13069.

[28] R. Feldt, F. Gomes, R. Torkar, Ways of applying artificial intelligence in software engineering, in: International Workshop on Realizing Artificial Intelligence Synergies in Software Engineering (RAISE), IEEE, 2018, pp. 35–41.

[29] D. Gonzalez, T. Zimmermann, N. Nagappan, The state of the ml-universe: 10 years of artificial intelligence and machine learning software development on GitHub, in: Proceedings of the 17th International Conference on Mining Software Repositories, MSR '20, Association for Computing Machinery, 2020, pp. 431–442.

[30] S. Tahvili, R. Pimentel, W. Afzal, M. Ahlberg, E. Fornander, M. Bohlin, sortes: A supportive tool for stochastic scheduling of manual integration test cases, Journal of IEEE Access 6 (2019) 1–19.

[31] B. Eberhardinger, A. Habermaier, W. Reif, Toward adaptive, self-aware test automation, in: 2017 IEEE/ACM 12th International Workshop on Automation of Software Testing (AST), 2017, pp. 34–37.

[32] G. Rothermel, R. Untch, C. Chu, Prioritizing test cases for regression testing, IEEE Transactions on Software Engineering 27 (10) (2001) 929–948.

[33] S. Yoo, M. Harman, Regression testing minimization, selection and prioritization: A survey, Software Testing, Verification and Reliability 22 (2) (2012) 67–120.

[34] S. Elbaum, A.G. Malishevsky, G. Rothermel, Test case prioritization: A family of empirical studies, IEEE Transactions on Software Engineering 28 (2) (2002) 159–182.

[35] M.R. Garey, D.S. Johnson, Computers and Intractability; A Guide to the Theory of NP-Completeness, W.H. Freeman and Co., USA, 1990.

[36] I. Porres, T. Ahmad, H. Rexha, S. Lafond, D. Truscan, Automatic exploratory performance testing using a discriminator neural network, in: 2020 IEEE International Conference on Software Testing, Verification and Validation Workshops (ICSTW), 2020, pp. 105–113.

[37] J. Chen, L. Zhao, M. Zhou, Y. Liu, S. Qin, An approach to determine the optimal k-value of k-means clustering in adaptive random testing, in: 2020 IEEE 20th International Conference on Software Quality, Reliability and Security (QRS), 2020, pp. 160–167.

[38] S. Shah, C. Gencel, U. Alvi, K. Petersen, Towards a hybrid testing process unifying exploratory testing and scripted testing, Journal of Software Maintenance and Evolution Research and Practice (February 2014).

[39] A. Lastovetsky, Parallel testing of distributed software, Information and Software Technology 47 (2005) 657–662.

[40] C. Landin, S. Tahvili, H. Haggren, M. Längkvist, A. Muhammad, A. Loutfi, Cluster-based parallel testing using semantic analysis, in: 2020 IEEE International Conference on Artificial Intelligence Testing (AITest), 2020, pp. 99–106.

[41] J. Jones, M. Harrold, Test-suite reduction and prioritization for modified condition/decision coverage, IEEE Transactions on Software Engineering 29 (3) (2003) 195–209.

[42] R. Abid, A. Nadeem, A novel approach to multiple criteria based test case prioritization, in: 2017 13th International Conference on Emerging Technologies (ICET), 2017, pp. 1–6.

[43] K. Wang, T. Wang, X. Su, Test case selection using multi-criteria optimization for effective fault localization, Computing 100 (8) (2018) 787–808.

## CHAPTER FIVE

Application of vectorized test artifacts

Chapter points

- This chapter provides comprehensive guidelines for conducting several industrial case studies at various levels of software testing.
- Several pipelines are provided for employing artificial intelligence and machine learning techniques for improving the testing process.
- A step-by-step guide is provided for empirical evaluation of the obtained results.
- Several industrial test optimization applications for the proposed solutions in this book are provided in this chapter.
- All the mentioned concepts in this book are exemplified by several industrial use cases in this chapter.

"It always seems impossible until it's done."

Nelson Mandela

The case study method is a learning technique that can help us face a particular industrial problem. Conducting industrial case studies facilitates the exploration of a real-world issue, helping us analyze and solve a defined problem using a variety of data sources [1]. By examining industrial case studies, we have the opportunity to develop and enhance various skills such as innovation and analytic skills. In this chapter, several case studies from Alstom Sweden AB and Ericsson AB, which are two large companies in Sweden, are presented. The main goal of selecting case studies from these two enterprises is to show how the proposed solutions in this book can be applied in the testing processes of two different domains. Alstom is focused on safety-critical systems and Ericsson's main focus is the telecommunications domain.

Since we are aware of the complexity and difficulty of data-gathering, problem definition, problem-solving, and empirical evaluation in the industry, we provide a step-by-step guide for each of the mentioned challenges. Moreover, as mentioned before, applying supervised and semi-supervised learning approaches requires having a labeled dataset, generating

Artificial Intelligence Methods for Optimization of
the Software Testing Process
https://doi.org/10.1016/B978-0-32-391913-5.00016-6

which might be a challenging and time-consuming process. Thus, we provide some samples of the questionnaires and surveys which have been successfully employed for data annotation.

5.1. Test artifact optimization using vectorization and machine learning

As explained in Chapter 2, the testing process can be performed manually, semi-automatically, or fully automatically. Based on the selected testing procedure, different test artifacts should be created and employed during the testing process. Some of the test artifacts such as requirements specification and test reports are a commonality in all testing procedures, where the way that the testing team designs and implements test cases varies based on the testing procedure.

Generally, test cases, requirements, test scripts, and test logs can be collectively called test artifacts. The number of required test artifacts for creating a successful testing process of a software product is a function of the following factors:

- the size and complexity of the software product;
- the testing level (e.g., unit, integration, system testing);
- the testing procedure (e.g., manual, automated);
- the maturity of the testing process.

Transforming the test artifacts into the embedding vectors can help the testing team to achieve more insight into them. For instance, the testing team can perceive the entire created requirements or test cases. Moreover, vectorizing the test artifacts can also lead to clues about the hidden relationships between them. This approach can guide the testing team to realize how many similar or identical test cases are created. We need to consider that in a large-scale software development environment, each of the mentioned test artifacts is going to be handled by a separate department, e.g., the requirement engineering section, test design section, and troubleshooting unit. Sometimes, the requirements are going to be divided based on the functionality, and in other cases, the requirements need to be managed based on the project delivery. Therefore, analyzing the test artifacts is a hard, time- and resource-consuming process, especially in large software development centers.

Table 5.1 presents a brief summary of the conducted industrial case studies in this book. In the upcoming sections, we analyze each of the

Table 5.1 A brief summary of the provided industrial case studies in this book.

Case study	Objective	Vectorization method	Machine learning method
1	Topic identification for the requirements specifications analysis using text vectorization and clustering	Sentence-Transformers	Agglomerative, K-means, K-medoids
2	Splitting up requirements into dependent and independent classes using text vectorization and classification	Sentence-Transformers	AutoKeras
3	Similarity and dependency detection between manual integration test cases using neural network embeddings and clustering	paragraph-vectors	HDBSCAN
4	Dividing manual integration test cases into dependent and independent classes using neural network embeddings and classification	paragraph-vectors	AutoKeras
5	Similarity detection between integration test scripts using neural network embeddings and classification	Code2Vec	AutoKeras
6	Clustering high-dimensional data points using HDBSCAN, t-SNE, and UMAP for similarity detection between integration test scripts	Code2Vec	HDBSCAN
7	Classifying log entries based on the failure causes using word representations and troubleshooting action classification	Log2Vec	AutoKeras
8	Log vector clustering using the HDBSCAN algorithm	Log2Vec	HDBSCAN

mentioned test artifacts and case studies from Table 5.1 separately. To ensure eligibility of the conducted case studies, our approach is inspired by the directions and guidelines that were set out by Runeson and Höst [2] and Tahvili [3].

5.2. Vectorization of requirements specifications

Requirements engineering is the process of eliciting stakeholders' demands and desires and developing them into an agreed–upon set of detailed requirements that can serve as a basis for all subsequent development activities. The purpose of the requirements engineering is to make the problem that is being stated clear and complete and to ensure that the solution is correct, reasonable, and effective [4]. Generally, the requirements are specified in a natural text (might be enriched text and non–controlled decipherable text). An example of a requirements specification is presented in Table 2.2.

Analyzing the text behind each requirements specification can provide valuable information which can be easily adopted for numerous test optimization purposes. The most common use of the requirements specifications is test case design and test case creation. Reading a requirements specification line by line provides a clue to what needs to be tested. Requirement analysis in an early stage of a testing process can help the testing team to create the test cases in a more efficient way. This optimization process can be performed in a number of forms such as classifying or clustering similar requirements, ranking the requirements for test case generation, merging, or eliminating some of the requirements.

In this section, two industrial case studies are presented. We investigate two different test optimization approaches using requirements specifications. The first case study looks at the requirements clustering using the topic identification model presented in Chapter 3. The main application of this case study is test case design and test case creation. The second case study is about classifying requirements specifications into dependent and independent classes. In this case study, the SBERT model is utilized for the vectorization of each requirements specification. The generated vectors are then processed using the AutoKeras model to determine an optimal classifier.

Fig. 5.1 shows our proposed pipeline for employing the requirements specification for several test optimization purposes. In this section, we also evaluate the feasibility of vectorizing the requirements specifications by conducting a ground truth survey at Alstom Sweden AB. Both case studies are performed on a manual testing process at the integration testing level.

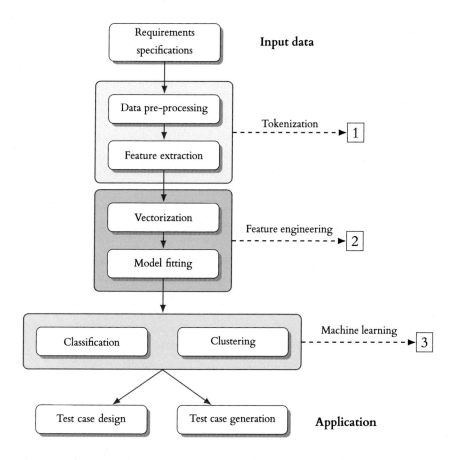

Figure 5.1 The proposed pipeline for vectorization of requirements specifications.

5.2.1 Unit of analysis and procedure for analyzing the requirements specifications

The cases under study are the requirements specifications designed for the Singapore R151 project.[1] The case studies are performed in several steps:

- The Singapore R151 project is selected as a case under study.
- A total number of 1527 requirements are extracted from the DOORS Next Generation database at Alstom for the Singapore R151 project.

---

[1] Alstom Sweden AB has signed an agreement with the Singapore Land Transport Authority to supply 6 additional Metropolis trains and 11 additional Metropolis trains for the extensions of the Singapore North-East Line and Circle Line, respectively.

- The text behind each requirements specification is pre-processed using the tokenization method.
- The pre-processed texts for the requirements specifications are used for the vectorization by employing the SBERT model, specifically all-MiniLM-L6-v2 from the SentenceTransformers package.
- The generated vectors by SBERT are later utilized for clustering using agglomerative, K-means, and K-medoids algorithms in Case Study 1 and classification using the AutoKeras model in Case Study 2.
- The obtained results are evaluated against the conducted ground truths which are presented in Appendix A.
- The results of classified and clustered requirements are presented to the Singapore R151 project team members at Alstom Sweden AB.

5.2.2 Case Study 1: Topic identification for the requirements specifications analysis using text vectorization and clustering

Table 5.2 Parameters and versions of packages used for Case Study 1.

Package	Version	Purpose	Parameters
Sentence-Transformers	2.1.0	Vectorization	The following pre-trained model is used: all-MiniLM-L6-v2
sklearn.cluster	1.0.2	Clustering	Default parameters.

As mentioned before, the requirements specifications are usually written in a natural text by the requirement engineering team. In order to provide a vector for each requirements specification, we employed the SBERT model (the detailed case study setup is presented in Table 5.2). As is well known, the output of the SBERT is a set of high-dimensional data points, which can be utilized for both clustering and classification purposes. In this case study, we aim to use topic identification and clustering for splitting the requirements into different clusters. Moreover, in order to evaluate and compare the performance of each clustering algorithm, (1) we utilized several clustering algorithms (agglomerative, k-means, and k-medoids), (2) the performance of each of the clustering algorithms is evaluated against a conducted ground truth at Alstom Sweden AB, and (3) the adjusted mutual information (AMI), normalized mutual information (NMI), and the adjusted rand index (ARI) are selected as performance metrics. As we reviewed earlier in this book, combining the topic identification and text document clustering provides an opportunity to group similar content documents from the collection. Since the input to Case Study 1 is the requirements specification, the obtained clusters consist of a group of requirements that are designed to complete a similar statement of what the system will do.

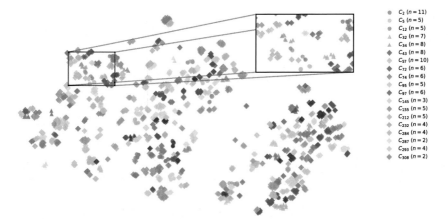

Figure 5.2 The clustered requirements specifications using the SBERT model for vectorization and the agglomerative algorithm for the clustering, where C represents the cluster number and n indicates the size of each cluster. The embeddings were dimensionally reduced using the t-SNE model.

Figs. 5.2, 5.3, and 5.4 visualize the achieved clusters using agglomerative, K-means, and K-medoids clustering algorithms, respectively, where the numbers of obtained clusters are different. Note that the input to all clustering algorithms is the generated vectors by the SBERT model on the requirements specifications. Moreover, the t-SNE model is employed for visualizing Figs. 5.2, 5.3, and 5.4.

Table 5.3 The obtained results for Case Study 1, where the requirements specifications are employed for the proposed machine learning pipeline in Fig. 5.1 against the ground truth.

	AMI	NMI	ARI
Agglomerative	0.902	0.970	0.794
K-Means	0.860	0.957	0.726
K-Medoids	0.664	0.883	0.468

Table 5.3 summarizes the performance evaluation of each clustering algorithm against the conducted ground truth at Alstom Sweden AB. The details of the ground truth are presented in Fig. A.1 in Appendix A.1.1. As we can see in Table 5.3, three different performance metrics (AMI, NMI,

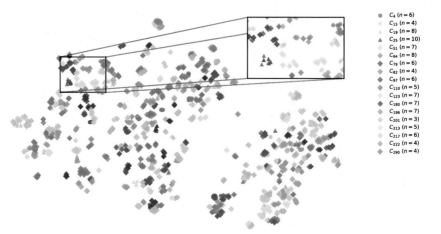

Figure 5.3 The clustered requirements specifications using SBERT for vectorization and the K-means algorithm for the clustering, where C represents the cluster numbers and n indicates the size of each cluster. The embeddings were dimensionally reduced using the t-SNE model.

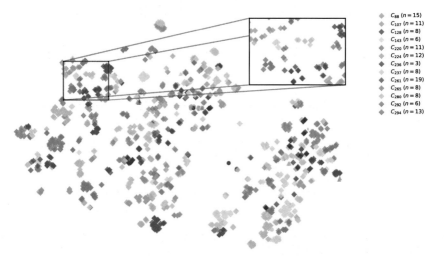

Figure 5.4 The clustered requirements specifications using SBERT for vectorization and the K-medoids algorithm for the clustering, where C represents the cluster numbers and n indicates the size of each cluster. The embeddings were dimensionally reduced using the t-SNE model.

and ARI) are selected for comparing the performance of each clustering algorithm. Based on the reported results in Table 5.3 the agglomerative hierarchical clustering algorithm shows the highest performance compared to other employed clustering algorithms. However, NMI generally provides a higher value compared to other performance metrics.

5.2.3 Optimization strategy and industrial application

As visualized in Figs. 5.2, 5.3, and 5.4 the 1527 requirements are divided into several clusters (average 297 clusters) using different clustering algorithms. The main aim of topic identification and document clustering is to group similar items. Therefore, the clustered requirements in Figs. 5.2, 5.3, and 5.4 should be topically similar to each other. The conducted ground truth in Appendix A.1.1 (see Fig. A.1) indicates the topics which are originally defined by the requirement engineering team for a train system at Alstom Sweden AB. Part of the mentioned topics is presented in Table 5.4.

Table 5.4 Some examples of the designed sub-level functional groups (SLFGs) at Alstom Sweden AB.

Number	Topic
1	Emergency ventilation
2	Manual external internal fire
3	Automatic internal smoke mode
4	Manual emergency ventilation
5	Air damper position

Even though each cluster includes similar requirements, dealing with a large set of clusters needs to be considered as well. In this subsection, we propose a set of cluster-based requirement-ranking strategies based on the topic similarity between the requirements. In fact, ranking the achieved clusters can help the testing team design and create the test cases for each requirement in a more structured way. The following definitions are applicable.

Definition 5.1. Let $C := \{C_1, C_2, \ldots, C_n\}$, where each C_j is a cluster and $j = 1, 2, \ldots, n$.

Let the cardinality of each C_j be K_j, where $K_j \in \mathbb{N}$ and $K_j > 1$. We define K_j as a cluster size.

The size of each cluster in Definition 5.1 represents the number of requirements per cluster in this case. Based on Definition 5.1, we can define several strategies for ranking the requirements for test case design and generation. However, each strategy has its own assumptions, benefits, disadvantages, and also limitations. Selecting a proper strategy for employing

Case Study 1 needs to be considered based on the testing team's goal, deadline, and infrastructure.

Strategy A: Increasing/decreasing prioritization for the clustered requirements

- **Assumptions.** (1) There are no dependencies between the requirements, which means each requirement can be selected for test creation separately. (2) All requirements have the same value for the test creation, denoting that there is no preferable requirement and all the requirements should be utilized for the test creation. In some companies, some requirements are more critical compared to other requirements. For instance, those requirements which are related to the "Temperature system" should be highly ranked and thereby the test cases which are associated with those requirements must be designed, created, and executed in an early stage of the testing process.
- **Solution.** If all the mentioned assumptions are satisfied, then cluster C_i has a higher priority to be ranked for test case creation than cluster C_j if and only if $K_i > K_j$, where $i, j \in 1, 2, \ldots, n$. This strategy can be called *increasingly ordering*. Strategy A can be defined as decreasingly ordering such that C_i has a higher priority than C_j if and only if $K_i < K_j$, where $i, j \in 1, 2, \ldots, n$. In other words, the clusters are ranked in strategy A based on their size. However, if two (or more) clusters have the same size $(K_i = K_j)$, then strategy A is not applicable and a new strategy should be considered.
- **Advantages, disadvantages, and limitations.** Applying strategy A can help the testing team to test a product faster, where those clusters of the requirements which have a larger size will be ranked higher for test case creation. However, strategy A has several assumptions, which makes it limited.

Strategy B: Requirement selection and cluster size reduction

- **Assumptions.** The existing requirements can be merged or removed; in other words, there are some requirements that can be merged with other requirements.
- **Solution.** As we see in Figs. 5.2, 5.3, and 5.4, the size of each cluster is different; sometimes more than 10 requirements are clustered together. Selecting a subset of requirements per cluster is the main aim of strategy B. In this regard, we need to know which requirement is a good candidate for test case creation. However, since the text behind

each requirement is available, we are able to measure the line of the text, calculate the percentage of similarity between the requirements, and highlight duplicates. Applying strategy B is beneficial especially in large industries, where a large number of requirements are designed by a team, which might include extremely similar and identical requirements specifications. Using strategy B can also help the testing team to design the requirements specification in a more efficient way in the future.

• **Advantages, disadvantages, and limitations.** Selecting a subset of requirements for test case design requires human work and judgment, which might be a time- and resource-consuming process and also suffers from ambiguity and uncertainty.

Finally, the main advantage of applying Case Study 1 in Section 5.2.2 is the way that we solve the problem without any labeled data. In fact, the patterns between requirements can be detected, which are not possible to find using normal methods.

5.2.4 Case Study 2: Splitting up requirements into dependent and independent classes using text vectorization and classification

One of the main assumptions which add limitations to the process of requirements selection and prioritization are the dependencies between the requirements.

Dependencies between requirements have a direct impact on the dependencies between test cases and their run sequences. There is a great variety of ways that the requirements can be described in the industry. There is therefore a risk that we faced requirements that exhibit strong functional dependencies on each other. Two requirements are functionally dependent on each other if they are interacting with the connected modules.[2] For instance, module 1 will be enabled if its required functions are already enabled by module 2, thus module 2 is dependent on the module 1. Consequently, all requirements and thereby test cases that are designed to test module 2 should be executed any time after module 1. Detecting the dependencies between requirements is a challenging task where different parts of a system under test such as software architecture need to be analyzed.

Fig. 5.5 visualizes the mesh graph of the dependencies between some of the requirements in the Singapore R151 project, where the blue nodes rep-

---

[2] A software module is a logical subset of the functionality provided by the software.

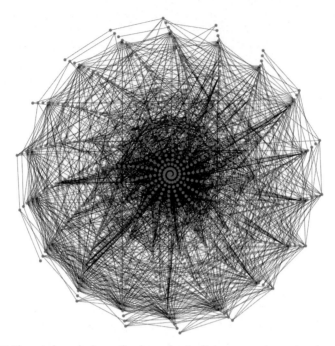

Figure 5.5 The spiral graph shows the dependencies between requirements, where the blue nodes represent requirements and the black lines indicate the dependencies between each requirement.

resent requirements and the black lines indicate the dependencies between each requirement. As we can see in Fig. 5.5, there are complex interdependencies between the requirements, which are not possible to be detected manually. In order to solve this issue, we designed Case Study 2, which aims to classify the requirements into dependent and independent classes. In this case study, we again utilize the Singapore R151 project, wherein a total of 1527 requirements are analyzed for dependency detection. Moreover, the presented information in Fig. 5.5 is a part of the conducted ground truth which will be used later for the performance evaluation. Note that the independent requirements are not presented in Fig. 5.5. More details regarding this ground truth can be found in Appendix A.1.2 and Fig. A.2. For conducting Case Study 2, a supervised learning approach is utilized. Since the dependencies between the requirements are detected from the software architecture (see Appendix A.1.2), we have this opportunity to train the presented model in Fig. 5.1 for the dependency detection.

In summary, the text behind each requirements specification is used for the vectorization applying the SBERT model; later via employing the

Table 5.5 Parameters and versions of packages used for Case Study 2.

Package	Version	Purpose	Parameters
Sentence-Transformers	2.1.0	Vectorization	The following pre-trained model is used: `all-MiniLM-L6-v2`
AutoKeras	1.0.16	Classification	Using StructuredDataClassifier with `max_trials=20`

AutoKeras model we classified the requirements into two main classes. The Python code for implementing AutoKeras can be found in Listing 5.6, and the details of the specific packages used are presented in Table 5.5.

Table 5.6 Summary of the obtained results for classifying the requirements specifications into dependent and independent classes against the ground truth.

Description	Class	Precision	Recall	F1-score	Support
Independent	0	0.92	0.97	**0.95**	532
Dependent	1	0.91	0.78	0.84	195
Accuracy				**0.92**	727
Macro avg		0.92	0.88	**0.90**	727
Weighted avg		0.92	0.92	0.92	727

Table 5.6 summarizes the obtained results for classifying requirements into dependent and independent classes, using precision, recall, and the F1-score as performance metrics. As we can see in Table 5.6, the model shows a higher performance for detecting independent requirements (F1-score = 0.95) compared to the dependent requirements (F1-score = 0.84). In order to obtain more insight into the model's ability, we visualize the achieved results in Fig. 5.6.

In fact, Fig. 5.6 visualizes the sensitivity and specificity of the proposed pipeline in Fig. 5.1, where we can observe the performance of the model for correct/incorrect dependency and independency detection of the requirements.

5.2.5 Applications of dependency detection between requirements

As mentioned in this section, the application of the requirement vectorization is test design. Splitting all requirements into two main classes helps the testing team to identify those requirements which have a more complex dependency. Contrarily those requirements which are independent might require less time and effort to be used for test case design and creation.

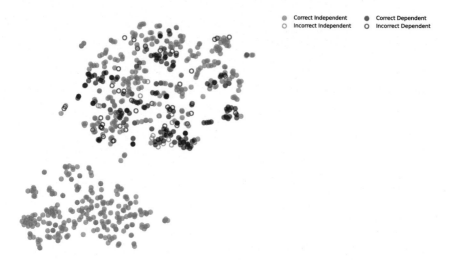

| ● Correct Independent | ● Correct Dependent |
| ○ Incorrect Independent | ○ Incorrect Dependent |

Figure 5.6 A visualized summary of the presented results in Table 5.6 for classifying the requirements specifications into dependent and independent classes against the ground truth.

Note that ranking the requirements specifications such as all other test artifacts should be considered as a multi–criterion decision-making problem. Other critical criteria (if any exist) should be added to the problem. In Case Study 2 we are just aiming to classify the dependent and independent requirements, where identifying and measuring the impact of other criteria is out of the scope of this case study. Finally, detecting the direction of dependencies between requirements (one-to-one connection) can be handheld manually or the dependent class of the requirements can be split into smaller classes. But the independent class does not require any further analysis.

5.3. Vectorization of test case specifications

A testing team generally consists of experts such as project managers, test analysts, test designers, testers, troubleshooters, and test developers who are dedicated to ensuring the best quality of software products. The testing team is also responsible for making sure the software product meets all the requirements. As soon as the requirements engineering team releases the requirements, the process of test design and test creation will be started. The main task of the testing team is to detect and solve the hidden defects and bugs inside a software product. The size of the testing team is related to the product complexity and also the maturity of the testing

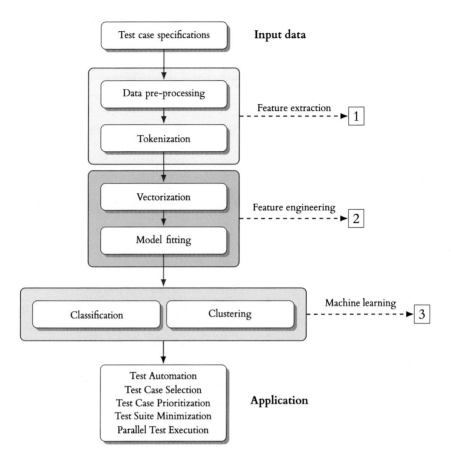

Figure 5.7 The proposed pipeline for vectorization of test case specifications.

process. As we know now, the testing process can be performed manually, semi-automatically, or fully automatically, where each of those approaches requires different test artifacts. In this section, we provide two industrial case studies for detecting the dependencies between manual integration test cases. An example of a test specification is already presented in Table 2.3, where a large set of the presented text in Table 2.3 is used for dependency detection. The main application of the case studies in this section is test case selection, prioritization, and test scheduling. For conducting both case studies, the Doc2Vec model is utilized for vectorization, where the generated vectors for each test specification are clustered using the HDBSCAN algorithm for Case Study 3. In Case Study 4 a supervised learning approach is applied via classifying all test cases into two classes using the AutoKeras model. Fig. 5.7 shows our proposed pipeline for employing the test specification for different test optimization purposes. In this section, we also evaluate the feasibility of vectorizing the test specifications by conducting a ground truth analysis at Alstom Sweden AB.

5.3.1 Unit of analysis and procedure for analyzing the manual test cases

The cases under study are the test specifications that are designed for the BR490 project[3] and the Singapore R151 project. The case studies are performed in several steps:

- The BR490 project and the Singapore R151 project are selected as cases under study.
- A total number of 1748 test specifications are extracted from the DOORS Next Generation database at Alstom Sweden AB for the BR490 project for conducting Case Study 3.
- A total number of 691 test specifications are extracted from the DOORS Next Generation database at Alstom for the Singapore R151 project for conducting Case Study 4.
- The text behind each test specification is pre-processed using the tokenization method for both case studies.
- The pre-processed texts for the test specifications are used for the vectorization via employing the Doc2Vec model in both case studies.
- The generated vectors by Doc2Vec are later utilized for clustering using the HDBSCAN algorithm for Case Study 3.
- The generated vectors by Doc2Vec are later utilized for classification using the AutoKeras model for Case Study 4.
- The obtained results are evaluated against the ground truths which are presented in Appendix A.1.3 and Appendix A.1.4.
- The results of the clustered and classified dependent and independent test cases are presented to the BR490 project and the Singapore R151 project team members at Alstom Sweden AB.

---

[3] The BR series is an electric rail car specifically designed for the S-Bahn Hamburg GmbH network in production at the Alstom Sweden AB facility. The heating system in the BR490 project is designed to use waste heat from the traction equipment system to heat the passenger compartment.

5.3.2 Case Study 3: Similarity and dependency detection between manual integration test cases using neural network embeddings and clustering

As we explained in Section 5.2.4 (and also described with details in Appendix A.1.2), the dependencies between requirements have a direct impact on the test case execution. In other words, if two requirements are dependent on each other, then all created test cases that will cover those requirements are also dependent on each other. Paying no attention to the dependencies between test cases might lead to unnecessary failures in a test execution process. Our research shows that up to 40% of the test executions can fail due to ignoring the dependencies [5] between test cases. Having a cluster of dependent and independent test cases can help the testing team to schedule the test cases for the execution properly. Versions and packages used for Case Study 3 are presented in Table 5.7.

Table 5.7 Parameters and versions of packages used for Case Study 3.

Package	Version	Purpose	Parameters
paragraph-vectors	N/A	Vectorization	Number of noise words 2, vector dimensions 128, batch size 32, and learning rate 0.001
HDBSCAN	0.8.27	Clustering	Using L2 normalization of the feature vectors to approximate cosine similarity.

As the number of required test cases for testing a software product increases, we will face more challenges for dependency detection. On the other hand, in a manual testing procedure, the test specification will be written by several members of the testing team. During the test design and creation, each team member is using his/her own proficiency of testing and language knowledge for describing the test activities. Although in some companies, a pre-defined template exists for test case creation, those kinds of documents are still suffering from human work, ambiguity, and uncertainty. One solution for reducing the human work for test creation is employing the text generator models such as in Fig. 3.11. Clustering the dependent and similar test cases can easily be adapted for daily test case scheduling, test case selection, and prioritization. Moreover, those clusters can also be used for test automation and test suite reduction. On the other hand, two test cases can be considered as similar if (1) they require the same system setup, installation, pre-conditions, or post-conditions or (2) they are

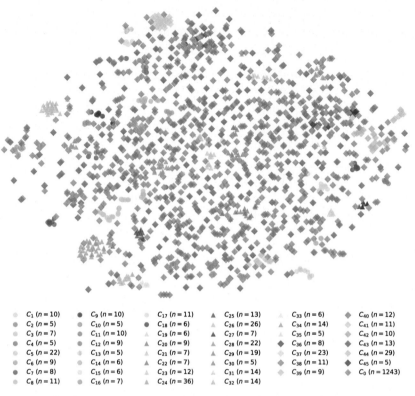

C_1 ($n = 10$)	C_9 ($n = 10$)	C_{17} ($n = 11$)	C_{25} ($n = 13$)	C_{33} ($n = 6$)	C_{40} ($n = 12$)
C_2 ($n = 5$)	C_{10} ($n = 5$)	C_{18} ($n = 6$)	C_{26} ($n = 26$)	C_{34} ($n = 14$)	C_{41} ($n = 11$)
C_3 ($n = 7$)	C_{11} ($n = 10$)	C_{19} ($n = 6$)	C_{27} ($n = 7$)	C_{35} ($n = 5$)	C_{42} ($n = 10$)
C_4 ($n = 5$)	C_{12} ($n = 9$)	C_{20} ($n = 9$)	C_{28} ($n = 22$)	C_{36} ($n = 8$)	C_{43} ($n = 13$)
C_5 ($n = 22$)	C_{13} ($n = 5$)	C_{21} ($n = 7$)	C_{29} ($n = 19$)	C_{37} ($n = 23$)	C_{44} ($n = 29$)
C_6 ($n = 9$)	C_{14} ($n = 6$)	C_{22} ($n = 7$)	C_{30} ($n = 5$)	C_{38} ($n = 11$)	C_{45} ($n = 5$)
C_7 ($n = 8$)	C_{15} ($n = 6$)	C_{23} ($n = 12$)	C_{31} ($n = 14$)	C_{39} ($n = 9$)	C_0 ($n = 1243$)
C_8 ($n = 11$)	C_{16} ($n = 7$)	C_{24} ($n = 36$)	C_{32} ($n = 14$)		

Figure 5.8 The clustered test case specifications for the BR490 project using the Doc2Vec model and HDBSCAN, where C_0 represents independent (or non-similar) test cases and n indicates the size of each cluster. The embeddings were dimensionally reduced using the t-SNE model.

designed to test the same or similar functions. Detecting the similarities between test cases can be performed via applying topic identification and also clustering such as in Case Study 1 in Section 5.2.2.

Fig. 5.8 visualizes the obtained results for clustering manual integration test cases. As we can see in Fig. 5.8, in total 45 clusters are formed, where the number of test cases inside each cluster is presented as n. In fact, the test cases which are clustered together are dependent and similar to each other, wherein a total of 1243 test cases are identified as independent and non–similar test cases (see cluster C_0 in Fig. 5.8).

It is obvious from Fig. 5.8 that the original utilized dataset in Case Study 3 suffers from unbalanced data. In total, the number of independent and non–similar test cases is higher than the number of dependent and similar test cases. This issue should be considered for the performance evaluation of Case Study 3. As in other presented case studies in this book, ground truth analysis was carried out at Alstom Sweden AB. In this regard, the dependencies between software modules, requirements, and test cases were detected by us by analyzing the system architecture for the BR490 project. Figs. A.3 and A.4 in Appendix A illustrate more details and the way how this ground truth is managed. The feasibility of the proposed solution in Case Study 3 is evaluated against the ground truth using precision, recall, the F1-score, and accuracy as performance metrics.

Table 5.8 A summary of the performance evaluation against ground truth for clustering the dependent and independent test case specifications, using the BR490 project at Alstom Sweden AB.

Description	Precision	Recall	F1-score	Accuracy
Original dataset	0.17	0.23	0.17	1.00
Subsampled dataset	1.00	0.23	0.75	0.61

A summary of the performance evaluation is provided in Table 5.8. These results were achieved using parameters specified in Table 5.7. As we can see, the F1-score for the original dataset is not impressive (F1-score = 0.17) due to the imbalanced data. However, applying random under-sampling on the original dataset improves the value of the F1-score significantly (F1-score = 0.75). In fact, Case Study 3 is a good example of the impact of imbalanced data on the machine learning models' performance evaluation. As stated before, choosing a proper performance metric especially when we are dealing with an imbalanced dataset is very important. However, by observing the obtained values for the accuracy in Table 5.8, we can see that on the original dataset we achieved accuracy ≈ 1, which does not indicate that the model has a perfect performance. This circumstance is known as the "accuracy paradox", where each example of the minority classes has a corresponding 100 example for the majority classes. On the other hand, monitoring the value of the accuracy on the subsampled data shows that the accuracy is decreased down to 0.61. In summary, the F1-score, AUC, and ROC are the recommended metrics for the performance evaluation in imbalanced datasets.

5.3.3 Applications of dependency and similarity detection between manual integration test cases

Two main optimization strategies can be applied using the results of Case Study 3. As mentioned before, the test cases inside of each cluster are semantically similar to each other, due to the usage of text vectorization and clustering. On the other hand, as is proved in Table 5.8, there is a dependency between the clustered test cases as well. In this subsection, we discuss how each of the mentioned applications can be employed for test optimization purposes.

Strategy 1: Parallel test execution of similar test cases

Executing similar test cases in one test station can help us save time for system setup, installation, test environment preparation, and pre-condition settings. As mentioned before, similar test cases are designed to test the same or similar functions, where they require the same system setup. Clustering similar test cases based on their test specifications and descriptions is one way to identify the similarities between them. However, in order to execute similar test cases inside of each cluster, several conditions need to be met.

- **Assumptions.** (1) All test cases have the same value for execution. (2) There are enough available test stations to make parallel testing possible.
- **Solution.** The achieved clusters can be ranked on the different test stations based on the size of each cluster. Both increasing and decreasing execution orders are applicable in this case, which needs to be aligned to the company policies. If we have to execute as many test cases as possible during working hours, and then selecting a big-size cluster that includes similar test cases can be beneficial. In fact, we prepare the test station once, and later several test cases are going to be executed after each other in this test station. Furthermore, since all non–similar test cases are gathered inside of one cluster, we have this opportunity to rank them for execution at the end of the testing cycle.
- **Advantages, disadvantages, and limitations.** The main advantage of this strategy is minimizing the system setup installation time. Moreover, monitoring the test execution results is another advantage of employing the parallel test execution, where the failed test cases can be troubleshot more easily and faster due to the similarity of the tested function by each of them. Note that we are just considering the similarity between test cases for ranking them for execution. It might be the case that some test cases have a higher value, priority for the execution, e.g., they required less time for execution or they have a higher requirement coverage compared to other test cases. Parallel test execution generally requires a set of available test stations, where each cluster or a combination of the several clusters needs to be executed in one test station. Other clusters or non-similar clusters can be tested parallel

with each other on the other available test stations. In summary, this strategy is feasible for large enterprises which can provide the required infrastructures.

Strategy 2: Test execution scheduling and test automation using the dependency information between test cases

Ignoring the dependencies between test cases has a big impact on the usage of the testing resources. Several test failures can occur without providing any clue of the hidden bugs in the software product. In this strategy, the clustered test cases in Fig. 5.8 will be utilized for scheduling the test execution.

- **Assumptions.** The main assumption for applying this optimization strategy is the value for each test case. In this strategy, we assume that all test cases have the same value and cost for execution.
- **Solution.** Since we have a set of clusters of dependent test cases and one cluster of independent test cases, we can decide which cluster should be executed first. As with the previous strategy, the size of each cluster can be considered as an important factor for ranking the clusters for execution. Moreover, as we know, besides the dependencies between test cases, those test cases which are clustered together are also similar to each other as well. Therefore, test automation can be considered as another application of this strategy. Since the manual integration test cases are utilized for this case study, a subset of the provided cluster by the machine learning model can be selected for test automation. One criterion for test automation can be the complexity of the dependencies between test cases. If we have a long chain of dependent test cases, then they might be good candidates for test automation. However, the independent test cases whose execution results have no impact on the other test cases can remain for the manual test execution.
- **Advantages, disadvantages, and limitations.** Dynamic test scheduling is the main advantage of this strategy. Ranking a cluster of the dependent test cases can help the testing team to select which test case of the cluster should be executed first. As we explained, the dependent test cases have a direct impact on each other, which means that in case of a failure inside a cluster, another cluster can be ranked for execution. In other words, if one test case inside a cluster fails during the test execution, other dependent test cases in that cluster might fail after each other. Dynamically monitoring the test execution results and decision-making based on that can significantly minimize the testing

cost via avoiding unnecessary failures during the test execution process. The proposed solution in Case Study 3 just provides several clusters of the dependent test cases. However, the one-to-one dependency between test cases inside of each cluster needs to be checked manually. Although this process is manual, a lower number of test cases need to be analyzed by the testing team. In fact, the first step of splitting test cases based on the dependencies is performed by the proposed machine learning model. As shown in Fig. 5.8, the number of test cases per cluster is limited compared to the original dataset and can easily be handled manually.

5.3.4 Case Study 4: Dividing manual integration test cases into dependent and independent classes using neural network embeddings and classification

Having a labeled dataset provides the opportunity to apply a supervised learning approach for dependency and similarity detection between manual integration test cases. In order to show the feasibility and generalizability of the proposed pipeline in Fig. 5.7, the Singapore R151 project is selected for performing Case Study 4. The text behind 691 text specifications is inserted into the Doc2Vec model for vectorization. Later the obtained vectors are clustered using the AutoKeras model into two classes which can be interpreted as a dependent and similar class and an independent and non–similar class. The dependency between the test cases is checked via analyzing the signal communication between the software modules for the Singapore R151 project. More details regarding the performed ground truth analysis for Case Study 4 are presented in Appendix A.1.4 and Fig. A.5.

For the performance evaluation of Case Study 4 against the ground truth, the confusion matrix including precision, recall, and F1–score is selected. Table 5.9 summarizes the obtained results of the supervised learning combining Doc2Vec and the AutoKeras model for splitting up test cases into two main classes.

As we can see in Table 5.9, the proposed pipeline in Fig. 5.7 shows a higher performance for independent test cases (F1–score = 0.95) compared to its ability to detect the dependent test cases (F1–score = 0.47). Fig. 5.9 visualizes the ability of the proposed pipeline in Fig. 5.7 to divide test cases into two classes.

The same applications provided in Section 5.3.2 are valid in Case Study 4 as well.

Table 5.9 The obtained results for classifying the test case specification into dependent and independent classes employing the proposed machine learning pipeline in Fig. 5.7 against the ground truth in the Singapore R151 project.

Description	Class	Precision	Recall	F1-score	Support
Independent	0	0.94	0.96	**0.95**	182
Dependent	1	0.53	0.42	0.47	19
Accuracy				**0.91**	201
Macro avg		0.74	0.69	**0.71**	201
Weighted avg		0.90	0.91	0.91	201

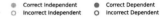

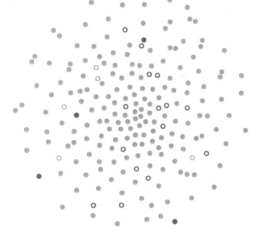

Figure 5.9 The classified test case specifications into independent and dependent classes using Doc2Vec and the AutoKeras model. This figure corresponds to the results presented in Table 5.9.

5.4. Vectorization of test scripts

Test automation is a recommended testing procedure in terms of time efficiency. Sometimes, during a testing process, a test case needs to be executed several times, thus having a test script that can be executed automatically reduces the manual work. One of the main differences between manual and automated testing procedures is test case creation and execution. Contrary to manual test case creation and execution, test automation provides an opportunity for the testing team to generate the test cases and also execute them automatically. Although test automation is a time-efficient approach, the required time for generating, maintaining, and debugging test scripts might be high. Therefore using manual testing is still demanded in some industries.

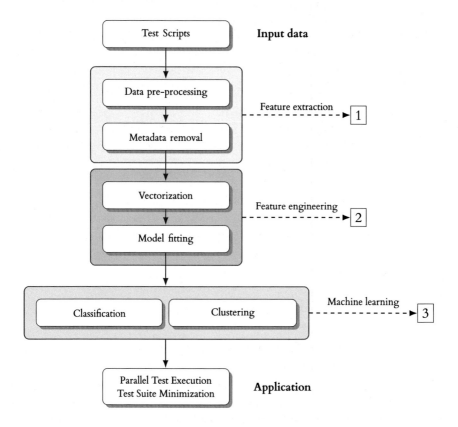

Figure 5.10 The proposed pipeline for vectorization of test scripts.

However, the issue of generating a large set of test scripts is also valid in test automation. Most of the test scripts (as presented in Chapter 2) are written in the same programming language as the code that they are testing, such as Java or C#, where in order to analyze them the testing team needs to have special proficiency and expertise. Unlike the test specifications which can be read and analyzed by the testing team, the process of code reviewing demands a supporting tool or experts. In this section, we propose a pipeline for applying a pre-trained machine learning model called Code2Vec for extracting the main functionality of the test scripts written in Java. The steps of the proposed pipeline are shown in Fig. 5.10. As shown in Fig. 5.10, test scripts are the input to the model, where via utilizing the pre-trained version of the Code2Vec model, we are able to derive corresponding vectors for each test script from a relatively small dataset. The utilized version of the Code2Vec model is already presented in Section 3.3.5 and Fig. 3.24, where our proposed algorithms for handling the vectors are added by us to Fig. 3.24. The original Code2Vec model is already trained on several large open-source Java projects (see [6]). As highlighted in Fig. 5.10 the obtained vectors of the Code2Vec model can be employed for both clustering and classification approaches. In this section, we combine the Code2Vec embeddings with the AutoKeras model for the classification and later with the HDBSCAN algorithm for the clustering. However, other methods for supervised or unsupervised learning can be adopted. Furthermore, the performance of both mentioned combinations is evaluated against a ground truth analyzed by the subject matter experts at Ericsson AB. An example of the utilized surveys is provided in Appendix A.1.5 and Table A.1.

5.4.1 Unit of analysis and procedure for analyzing the test scripts

The cases under study are an ongoing testing project at Ericsson AB. The unit of analysis is a test script that is designed for the integration testing level. The case studies are performed in several steps:

- An ongoing testing project is selected as a case under study.
- A total number of 102 test scripts consisting of one or several test functions are extracted from an internal database in Ericsson AB. In total, 736 test functions are identified.
- For the data pre-processing we removed the comments and metadata from each test script, using our custom implementation.
- The pre-processed test functions are utilized as input to the Code2Vec model.
- A set of high-dimensional data points corresponding to the test functions are generated by the Code2Vec model.
- The vectors provided by Code2Vec are used for classifying the similar test functions using the AutoKeras model in Case Study 5.
- The vectors provided by Code2Vec are later used for clustering the similar test functions via applying the HDBSCAN algorithm in Case Study 6.
- t-SNE and UMAP are applied for both dimensionality reduction and visualization in Case Study 6.

- The results of the identified similar test scripts are evaluated against the labeled data and also presented to the project team members at Ericsson AB.

5.4.2 Case Study 5: Similarity detection between integration test scripts using neural network embeddings and classification

In this case study, we have the intention to identify similar test scripts using their main functions via applying a code vectorization model. The utilized test scripts are written in Java code, where each test script might conceit several sub-functions and at least one main function. As stated before, a pre-trained version of Code2Vec is implemented, and in total 102 test scripts are selected as a testing set. Although the pre-trained version of the Code2Vec model shows promising results, the feasibility of the model needs to be evaluated in the conducted case study. Unlike the other presented case studies, we could not derive the ground truth by analyzing the software architecture. Through setting up several meetings with the subject matter experts at Ericsson AB, we realized that the testing team is manually selecting and ranking similar test scripts for the execution. The main reason behind this manual work is performing the troubleshooting process for similar test scripts effectively. In other words, the subject matter experts have insight regarding the generated similar test scripts. Therefore, we have decided to design a questionnaire and asked the testing team members to enter 0 for non-similar test scripts and 1 for similar test scripts. A sample of the questionnaire is presented in Table A.1 in Appendix A.1.5.

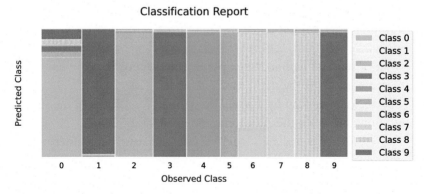

Figure 5.11 The obtained results of employing a supervised learning approach for classifying the test scripts. Those test scripts which are in the same class have the same main function.

The testing team needs to compare all test suites against each other, thus four different testers were nominated for this task. Fig. 5.11 shows the obtained results for classifying the entire test functions for the utilized test suites into 10 different classes. The provided classes in Fig. 5.11 indicate similar test scripts, which means that if two test scripts are grouped into the same class, then they have the same main function. As other advantages of classifying similar test artifacts, having a class or cluster of similar test scripts can help the testing team to rank the test cases for execution more efficiently.

As we can see in Fig. 5.11, the generated vectors by the Code2Vec model are divided into several classes where class 0 represents the uncategorized test scripts. Another usage of the generated vectors by the Code2Vec model is the possibility of deriving the main functionality of each test script. Each test script may contain additional sub-functions (functions that are only used to support the main testing function). Table 5.10 provides a brief excerpt of the number of sub-functions of some of the analyzed test scripts.

Table 5.10 Some examples of different functions within individual test scripts.

Script	# Function	Examples of functions
1	3	`BeforeBcConnection, BcProtocolRev1, AfterBcConnection`
2	5	`BeforeCarrierControlExceedingMaxDBCarrierPowerRejected,` `CarrierControlDBHighAndLowLevelPowerConfig,` `PrepareCarriersWithPowerGreaterThanApplicable,` `PrepareCarriersHighOrLowLevelPowerPorts,` `PrepareCarriersEqualPowerAllPorts`
3	4	`CarrierControlCheckDlBWBeforeClass,` `CarrierControlCheckDlBWBeforeMethod,` `CarrierControlCheckDlBWAfterMethod,` `CheckAllDlCarriersWithinDlBwBranch`

A brief look at the size of each class in Fig. 5.11 reveals that the original dataset is not balanced, which might be a challenge for the performance evaluation of the model. However, for conducting Case Study 5, we used a pre-trained model and we tested the model on a relatively small dataset, so an over-sampling solution was applied to the original dataset. The performance of the proposed pipeline in Fig. 5.10 is evaluated against the labeled data on the randomly over-sampled dataset. Table 5.11 provides a summary of the performance evaluation using precision, recall, and the F1-score as performance metrics.

Table 5.11 A summary of the performance evaluation for classifying the test scripts against the labeled data using the over-sampled dataset.

Class	Precision	Recall	F1-score
0	1	0.87	0.93
1	0.93	1	0.97
2	1	1	1
3	1	1	1
4	1	0.21	0.35
5	1	1	1
6	1	1	1
7	0.62	1	0.77
8	0.96	1	0.98
Accuracy			0.92
Macro avg	0.95	0.90	0.89
Weighted avg	0.94	0.92	0.90

As indicated in Table 5.11, the proposed pipeline for classifying the test scripts shows generally good performance for all classes except class 4. Moreover, achieving high precision in Table 5.11 implies that the proposed model returns more relevant results than irrelevant ones. In other words, most of the test scripts which are split up into one class are labeled as similar test scripts by the testing team as well.

5.4.3 Case Study 6: Clustering high-dimensional data points using HDBSCAN, t-SNE, and UMAP for similarity detection between integration test scripts

As hinted before, the generated vectors by the Code2Vec model can be clustered using a proper clustering algorithm. In Case Study 6 we apply the HDBSCAN algorithm, where similar functions across the test scripts can be divided into several clusters. One advantage of the HDBSCAN algorithm is the way that it is built for dealing with varying density datasets, and it is relatively fast. However, as we observed in other cases studies in this chapter, HDBSCAN provides a cluster of non–clusterable data points, which provides the possibility for identifying non–similar or independent test artifacts.

Fig. 5.12 visualizes the generated clusters by the HDBSCAN algorithm for clustering 763 data points, where each data point corresponds to a unique test function. The t-SNE model is applied in Fig. 5.12 for

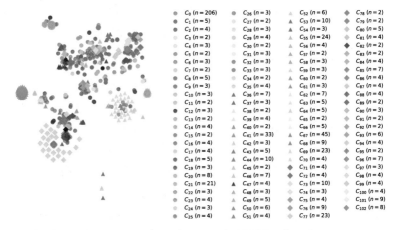

C_0 ($n=206$)	C_{26} ($n=3$)	C_{52} ($n=6$)	C_{78} ($n=2$)
C_1 ($n=5$)	C_{27} ($n=2$)	C_{53} ($n=10$)	C_{79} ($n=2$)
C_2 ($n=4$)	C_{28} ($n=3$)	C_{54} ($n=3$)	C_{80} ($n=5$)
C_3 ($n=2$)	C_{29} ($n=4$)	C_{55} ($n=24$)	C_{81} ($n=4$)
C_4 ($n=3$)	C_{30} ($n=2$)	C_{56} ($n=4$)	C_{82} ($n=2$)
C_5 ($n=2$)	C_{31} ($n=3$)	C_{57} ($n=2$)	C_{83} ($n=2$)
C_6 ($n=3$)	C_{32} ($n=3$)	C_{58} ($n=3$)	C_{84} ($n=4$)
C_7 ($n=2$)	C_{33} ($n=3$)	C_{59} ($n=3$)	C_{85} ($n=7$)
C_8 ($n=5$)	C_{34} ($n=2$)	C_{60} ($n=2$)	C_{86} ($n=4$)
C_9 ($n=3$)	C_{35} ($n=4$)	C_{61} ($n=3$)	C_{87} ($n=4$)
C_{10} ($n=3$)	C_{36} ($n=7$)	C_{62} ($n=7$)	C_{88} ($n=4$)
C_{11} ($n=2$)	C_{37} ($n=3$)	C_{63} ($n=5$)	C_{89} ($n=2$)
C_{12} ($n=3$)	C_{38} ($n=2$)	C_{64} ($n=5$)	C_{90} ($n=3$)
C_{13} ($n=2$)	C_{39} ($n=4$)	C_{65} ($n=2$)	C_{91} ($n=2$)
C_{14} ($n=4$)	C_{40} ($n=2$)	C_{66} ($n=5$)	C_{92} ($n=2$)
C_{15} ($n=2$)	C_{41} ($n=33$)	C_{67} ($n=45$)	C_{93} ($n=6$)
C_{16} ($n=4$)	C_{42} ($n=3$)	C_{68} ($n=9$)	C_{94} ($n=4$)
C_{17} ($n=4$)	C_{43} ($n=5$)	C_{69} ($n=23$)	C_{95} ($n=2$)
C_{18} ($n=5$)	C_{44} ($n=10$)	C_{70} ($n=4$)	C_{96} ($n=7$)
C_{19} ($n=3$)	C_{45} ($n=2$)	C_{71} ($n=4$)	C_{97} ($n=3$)
C_{20} ($n=8$)	C_{46} ($n=7$)	C_{72} ($n=4$)	C_{98} ($n=4$)
C_{21} ($n=21$)	C_{47} ($n=4$)	C_{73} ($n=10$)	C_{99} ($n=4$)
C_{22} ($n=3$)	C_{48} ($n=3$)	C_{74} ($n=3$)	C_{100} ($n=4$)
C_{23} ($n=4$)	C_{49} ($n=5$)	C_{75} ($n=4$)	C_{101} ($n=9$)
C_{24} ($n=3$)	C_{50} ($n=6$)	C_{76} ($n=9$)	C_{102} ($n=8$)
C_{25} ($n=4$)	C_{51} ($n=4$)	C_{77} ($n=23$)	

Figure 5.12 The clustered test script using Code2Vec and HDBSCAN, where C_0 represents non-clusterable data points and n indicates the size of each cluster. Embeddings are dimensionally reduced using the t-SNE model.

dimensionality reduction and visualization. As we can see, in total 206 unique test functions are identified as non-similar functions (see cluster C_0 in Fig. 5.12). Moreover, the remaining unique test functions are split into 102 clusters where the size of each cluster differs.

Employing the UMAP model for visualization and dimensionality reduction has its own advantages, e.g., UMAP is very fast and it can easily deal with large datasets and high-dimensional data. In this regard, the generated clusters by the HDBSCAN algorithm are also visualized using the UMAP model in Fig. 5.13.

The main reason for applying two different models for dimensionality reduction and visualization is that the readers observe the models' differences using the same dataset. As we can see in Fig. 5.12, the provided clusters by the t-SNE model are more uncrowded, whereas applying the UMAP model on the same dataset in Fig. 5.13 provides more compact clusters which can be potentially used to apply a variety of two-dimensional clustering methods.

For the performance evaluation of the provided clusters by the HDBSCAN model, we employed the labeled data and also accuracy, precision, recall, and the F1-score as performance metrics. As emphasized in Case Study 5, the initial problem suffers from an imbalance ratio, so a subsampling approach needs to be performed for evaluating the model. Table 5.12 provides a summary of the obtained values for each performance metric using the original imbalanced dataset and also the subsampled balanced

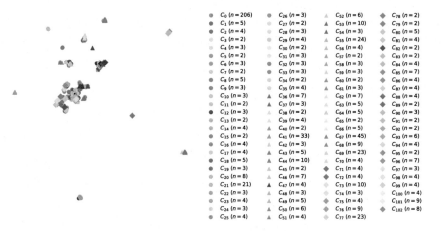

Figure 5.13 The clustered test script using Code2Vec and HDBSCAN, where C_0 represents non-clusterable data points and n indicates the size of each cluster. Embeddings are dimensionally reduced using the UMAP model.

Table 5.12 The performance metrics for evaluating the efficiency of the proposed pipeline for similarity detection between test scripts using Code2Vec and HDBSCAN. The performance of the utilized model is evaluated against the labeled data on both the original subsampled datasets.

Description	Accuracy	Precision	Recall	F1-score
Full dataset	0.54	0.07	1	0.13
Subsampled dataset	0.73	0.65	1	0.79

dataset. As we can observe in Table 5.12, the accuracy is higher than the F1-score on the original dataset which is imbalanced. This "accuracy paradox" situation usually happens on imbalanced datasets. Although the F1-score value is very low on the original dataset (F1-score = 0.13), applying a subsampling approach on the original dataset leads to a significant increase in the value of the F1-score (F1-score = 0.79). Moreover, after subsampling, we can observe a more harmonic relationship between the accuracy value (accuracy = 0.73) and the F1-score value (F1-score = 0.79). Finally, the obtained results on Case Study 6 can be considered as an example for choosing a proper performance metric and handling the imbalance ratio in the datasets.

5.4.4 Applications of similarity detection between test scripts

Since the grouped test scripts into the class or cluster are similar to each other, two main optimization strategies can be applied using the results of Case Studies 5 and 6. In this subsection, we discuss how each of the mentioned applications can be employed for test optimization purposes.

Strategy A: Parallel test execution

- **Assumptions.** (1) There is no dependency between test cases, where each test case can be executed separately and the test executions of the test cases have no impact on each other. (2) There are enough available test stations to make parallel testing possible.
- **Solution.** The obtained clusters (Fig. 5.12 and Fig. 5.13) can be scheduled for execution on several test stations based on the size of each cluster. Both increasing and decreasing execution orders are applicable in this case. Moreover, the achieved classes in Fig. 5.11 can also be ranked based on the class size or the degree of importance of each class, which needs to be assigned by the test managers. One criterion that can be considered for the degree of importance of the classes is the main function of each class.
- **Advantages, disadvantages, and limitations.** The main advantage of the parallel test execution in Case Studies 5 and 6 is accelerating the test execution, where several functions can be fully tested parallel with each other. In a sequence test execution, one function is divided into several test cases and it will be tested gradually, where it might take a while for a function to be fully tested. However, fully testing several functions can lead to a faster release of a software product. Another advantage of this strategy is related to the test stations preparation. The clustered or classified test scripts aim to test the same functionality, thus they might require the same system setup or installation. Although parallel testing requires an appropriate testing infrastructure, it significantly reduces testing teams' bug-fixing time. One of the obstacles of applying this strategy is the dependency detection process (if it exists between test cases), which should be performed manually.

Strategy B: Test suite minimization

Test suite reduction is another optimization scenario for Case Studies 5 and 6. A test suite might grow to such an extent that it is hard to execute all the test cases. This issue can directly impact the release date of a software product and also the testing resources. On the other hand, some test suites need to be executed repeatedly for every small change in the software; therefore, minimizing those test suites is beneficial in terms of time and cost.

- **Assumption.** (1) There are some test cases that will over-test a function. (2) There are some functions that do not need to be tested 100%.
- **Solution.** The size of the classes in Fig. 5.11 or clusters in Fig. 5.12 and Fig. 5.13 can be considered as a factor for this strategy. However, other criteria such as requirement coverage, execution time, and also dependency need to be investigated as well. To remove a single test script from a test suite, besides the similarities between the test script, we also need to check the value of this test script. This value can be added to the test cases by putting a number in advance. The numeric value for each test case can be the sum of, e.g., the number of the requirements which will be tested by this test case, or the execution time. Those factors can be extracted from the execution history. Another strategy for test suite minimization is monitoring the test coverage. As mentioned before, it might be the case that one function becomes over-tested. By monitoring the similarities between the classified or clustered test scripts, the testing team can realize which test script can be removed without impacting the test coverage. In some testing processes, it also might be the case that a function does not need to be tested 100%, thus it will be easier for the testing team to select the correct test case candidates for test suite minimization.
- **Advantages, disadvantages, and limitations.** The main benefit of test suite minimization is efficient usage of the testing resources and infrastructures. Having fewer test cases for execution requires limited test equipment and also the problem of unavailability of the testing station might be solved. Combining strategies A and B in this section is one of the optimal usages of the allocated resources which can increase the test coverage and thereby the quality of the final product. One of the barriers to applying this strategy is the demanded human knowledge and decision for selecting the correct test candidates for exclusion.

5.5. Vectorization of test logs

Test logs mostly contain information about the system, including the kernel, services, applications, errors, and exceptions that occurred during the test execution. The provided messages by the logs can facilitate the debugging process, analysis, and troubleshooting issues or monitor system functions. Generally, information and exceptions in each log are described in greater detail rather than the expected output details tab in a test case. To

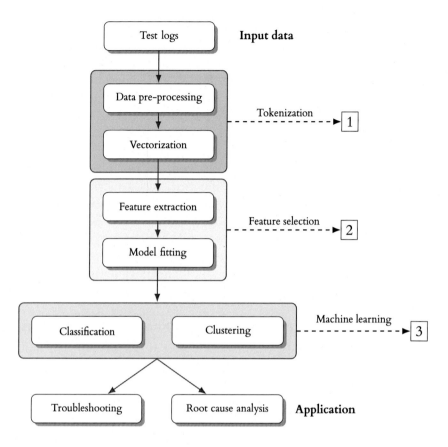

Figure 5.14 The proposed pipeline for vectorization of test logs.

extract meaningful data from logs, we need to engage some additional applications or management tools. Moreover, log analysis is not just limited to the troubleshooting activities, it can be also employed to pinpoint the root cause of application or system errors, as well as finding the trends and patterns to make better data-driven decisions. As the number of required test cases for testing a software product increases, more logs will be generated, since each test case might be executed several times.

In this section, we are proposing a new pipeline for log analysis using vectorization. The proposed pipeline illustrated in Fig. 5.14 can be applied for both classification and clustering. The main application of this pipeline is to facilitate troubleshooting activities. It is often the case that the testing systems log enormous quantities of data and that we first need to isolate the errors in logs that we will address. In this case study, the isolation was achieved by looking for specific keywords that indicate error messages (such as assertion failures) in the logs and then extracting the row containing that message as well as the five preceding messages. By doing this we are removing the irrelevant information that can introduce additional biases into the mode, such as station name, IP address, or time of the activity. We refer to this extracted subset as a log entry. As we can see in Fig. 5.14, log entries are the input to the model, where as in all other machine learning-based approaches, first the data need to be pre-processed. For the vectorization of the log entries, the presented Log2Vec model in Fig. 3.23 needs to be implemented. Since we are using real industrial data, we have decided to explore both supervised and unsupervised learning approaches. The required labeled data for supervised learning is a set of surveys conducted by three subject matter experts at Ericsson AB. The conducted surveys are used later as ground truth to evaluate the performance of the proposed pipeline illustrated in 5.14 for both classification and clustering. A sample of the mentioned surveys is presented in Table A.2 in Appendix A.1.6.

5.5.1 Unit of analysis and procedure for analyzing the test logs

The cases under study are an ongoing test project at Ericsson AB. The unit of analysis is log entries generated after test execution at the integration testing level. The case studies are performed in several steps:

- An ongoing testing project is selected as the case under study.
- A total of 548 log entries including information about the test execution are extracted from an internal database at Ericsson AB.
- Data pre-processing is performed via the embedded antonym and synonym extraction by the Log2Vec model.
- The pre-processed log entries are utilized as input for vectorization using the FastText model.
- In total, 32 log vectors are generated by the modified Log2Vec model where vectors are classified in Case Study 7 by the AutoKeras model and clustered using the HDBSCAN algorithm in Case Study 8.
- The feasibility of Case Studies 7 and 8 is evaluated against the gathered labeled data by the subject matter experts at Ericsson AB.

5.5.2 Case Study 7: Classifying log entries based on the failure causes using word representations and troubleshooting action classification

Reading, analyzing, and parsing the provided information inside each log entry has two main advantages: (1) mining the patterns and violations in a software product and (2) a faster troubleshooting process. As hinted previously, a test case might be executed several times at the different testing levels (or even at the same level) during the testing process. Therefore, generally, the number of log entries is larger than the number of test cases, where we face again the issue of manual analysis of a test artifact.

In order to map an appropriate troubleshooting activity for a failed test case, first, a troubleshooter needs to check the failure causes inside of a log report. In most of the log entries, this information is described textually. However, a log entry also consists of other information which might be irrelevant for the troubleshooting activities. Extracting the relevant information inside a log entry necessitates testing and root cause analysis skills.

Table 5.13 Some examples of the detected synonyms by the Log2Vec model for the test logs.

Word	Failed	Link	Port	Second	Set	Start	Verified
Synonym	fail	connection	interface	s	ready	get	assert

However, by applying new artificial intelligence methods, the troubleshooting team can first extract the relevant information from the logs. As presented in Chapter 3 and Fig. 3.23, during data pre-processing, the Log2Vec model automatically extracts synonyms and antonyms from the logs. Table 5.13 and Table 5.14 provide some examples of the detected synonyms and antonyms by the Log2Vec model on the utilized log entries in this case study.

Table 5.14 Some examples of the detected antonyms by the Log2Vec model for the test logs.

Word	Disabled	Expected	Saved	detaching	disabled	False	found
Antonym	enable	unexpected	lost	attach	enable	True	lost

The provided synonyms and antonyms in Table 5.13 and Table 5.14 can help the model to faster parse the log entries. In fact, the embedded data pre-processing in the Log2Vec is in conjunction with a word net-based model to extract the provided information in Table 5.13 and Table 5.14.

As shown in the proposed pipeline in Fig. 5.14, the pre-processed data will be used for vectorization. A sample of the generated vectors by Log2Vec is presented in Table 5.15.

The presented log vectors in Table 5.15 can now be utilized for both classification and clustering purposes. In the upcoming subsection, we evaluate the performance of the obtained results against the ground truth. As we can see in Table 5.15, 32 vectors are generated for the 548 log en-

Table 5.15 A sample of the obtained vectors for the log entries. In total 32 dimensions are derived for each log entry.

Log number	Vector 1	Vector 2	Vector 3	⋯	Vector 32
1	−0.106	−0.131	−0.537	⋯	0.022
2	−0.106	−0.131	−0.537	⋯	0.022
3	−0.106	−0.131	−0.537	⋯	0.022
4	−0.106	−0.131	−0.537	⋯	0.022
⋮	⋮	⋮	⋮	⋯	⋮
548	−0.397	−0.221	−0.105	⋯	−0.203

tries. The presented log vectors in Table 5.15 now can be utilized for both classification and clustering purposes.

As stated before, Case Study 7 aims to classify the log entries based on their required troubleshooting actions. In this regard, four classes of the high-level failure causes and troubleshooting activities have been defined by the troubleshooters at Ericsson AB. Through a survey analysis, the troubleshooters assigned each of the log entries into one of the mentioned classes via analyzing the failure causes in the log report. Moreover, class 0 is defined for the unknown failure causes, where those log reports which do not belong to the other four classes will be gathered in class 0.

Table 5.16 An example of the high-level troubleshooting causes for each class of the log entries. Class 0 is assigned for the unknown failure causes.

Class	Failure causes	Troubleshooting action
0	Unknown	More info is required
1	Environment issue	Action A
2	Authentication failed	Action B
3	Previous test case clean–up not done correctly	Action C
4	UE power on/off failure	Action D

Table 5.16 summarizes some of the high-level failure causes where a separated troubleshooting action is assigned for each class. Note that due to the stakeholder's request the actual troubleshooting actions are eliminated from Table 5.16, where they are replaced with Action A to D. However, since the proposed solution is not limited to the Telecom use cases, any other action can be specified for the failed test cases. For classifying the generated log vectors, the AutoKeras model is implemented which is a neural network-based classifier. Fig. 5.15 visualizes the obtained results for classifying log entries into five classes.

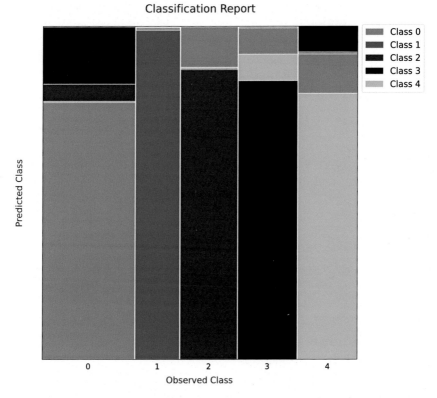

Figure 5.15 Results of supervised classification of log entries using the Log2Vec model and AutoKeras.

We need to consider that the entirety of the testing subset of data is represented by their ground truth and predicted classifications. The data is presented in Fig. 5.15 using a mosaic plot proposed by Michael Friendly [7]. As stated before, three different subject matter experts participated in conducting the ground truth analysis. We asked them to label log reports manually into mentioned classes based on the failure causes' similarity. The similarity, in this case, means that if two test cases failed based on the same failure causes reported in their log entries, then they required the same troubleshooting activities. The results of the performance evaluation for the proposed supervised learning (a combination of Log2Vec and the AutoKeras model with 25% of the dataset used as testing dataset) is summarized in Table 5.17 using precision, recall, and the F1-score.

As we can see in Table 5.17, the value of the F1-score is impressive for classes 1, 3, and 4, and the model also achieved a high value for the

Table 5.17 The results of the performance evaluation on the 25% of the dataset for classifying log entries against the labeled data.

Description	Class	Precision	Recall	F1-score	Support
	0	0.80	0.78	0.79	41
	1	0.92	0.88	0.90	25
	2	0.71	0.85	0.77	26
	3	0.91	0.81	0.86	26
	4	1.00	1.00	1.00	19
Accuracy				0.85	137
Macro avg		0.87	0.86	0.86	137
Weighted avg		0.85	0.85	0.85	137

F1-score for class 0, which indicates the unknown failure causes. Although the manual labeling of the log entries might be time-consuming, the data labeling will be performed once, where a large set of log entries can be classified based on their failure causes in a fraction of seconds.

5.5.3 Case Study 8: Log vector clustering using the HDBSCAN algorithm

Due to the manual data labeling by the troubleshooters in Case Study 7, we decided to apply an unsupervised learning approach in Case Study 8, where we can compare it with supervised learning.

Considering all advantages of supervised learning, however, it might be the case that collecting labeled data for running supervised learning requires a lot of resources for some industries. In this regard, in Case Study 8 we examine the performance of an unsupervised learning approach, which can be a combination of Log2Vec and any other clustering algorithm. Case Study 8 has the same steps as Case Study 7, where instead of classifying the log vectors, we apply the HDBSCAN algorithm for clustering them. In Fig. 5.16 we provide the obtained results for clustering the log entries into several clusters using one of the conducted surveys by the troubleshooters (Survey 3).

Fig. 5.16 visualizes the generated clusters by the HDBSCAN algorithm, where the t-SNE model is employed for both dimensionality reduction and visualization. Moreover, changing just the model for the dimensionality reduction and valuation to the UMAP model, Fig. 5.17 is obtained. As we can see in both Fig. 5.16 and Fig. 5.17, a total of 51 clusters are

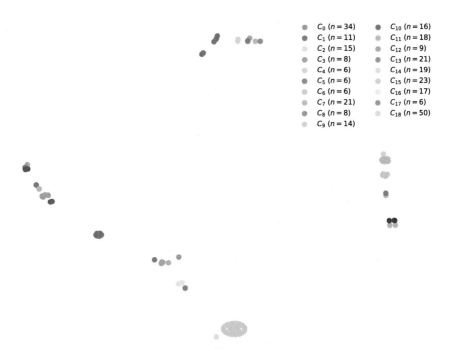

Figure 5.16 The clustered log entry using Log2Vec and the HDBSCAN algorithm using Survey 3, where C_0 represents non-clusterable data points and n indicates the size of each cluster. Embeddings are dimensionally reduced using t-SNE.

generated by the HDBSCAN algorithm, wherein a total of 34 log entries belong to the non–clusterable data points (see cluster C_0 in Fig. 5.16 and Fig. 5.17).

For the performance evaluation of Case Study 8, the labeled data by the troubleshooters is employed. A summary of the results is presented in Table 5.18 using accuracy, precision, recall, and F1-score. However, as we can see in Fig. 5.16 and Fig. 5.17, the size of each cluster is different, which implies the impacted dataset. In this regard, a subsampling approach is applied to the original dataset, where the mentioned confusion metrics are also evaluated on the subsampled dataset, reported in Table 5.18.

Casting a quick look at the summarized results in Table 5.18, we observe that (1) the subsampling approach slightly increased the F1–score value, (2) the accuracy is high due to the imbalanced dataset, and (3) the achieved value for precision is almost acceptable in all three surveys. The high value for precision implies the results from repeated measurements are close to each other in a cluster.

Table 5.18 A summary of the performance metrics on the full and subsampled dataset against the labeled data.

Survey	Row size	Dataset	TP	FP	TN	FN	Accuracy	Precision	Recall	F1-score
1	166	Full	1106	60	11023	1506	0.88	0.94	0.42	0.58
		Subsampled	1106	15	2584	1506	0.70	0.98	0.42	0.59
2	65	Full	102	71	952	415	0.68	0.58	0.19	0.29
		Subsampled	102	35	482	415	0.56	0.74	0.19	0.31
3	322	Full	2363	518	39119	6828	0.84	0.82	0.25	0.39
		Subsampled	2363	107	9096	6828	0.62	0.95	0.25	0.40

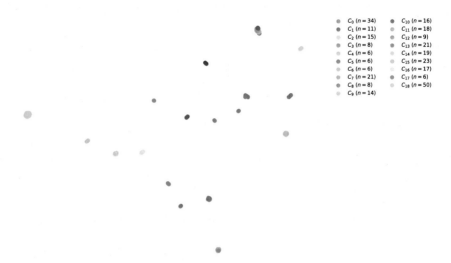

Figure 5.17 The clustered log entry using Log2Vec and HDBSCAN is based on Survey 3, where C_0 represents non-clusterable data points and n indicates the size of each cluster. Embeddings are dimensionally reduced using UMAP.

5.5.4 Applications of the test log vectorization

Grouping similar log entries based on the same failure cases of the executed test cases can provide a clue of the required same troubleshooting actions. Generally, a troubleshooter needs to read the entire log entry and use her/his knowledge for mapping proper troubleshooting activities. Those activities could be high-level activities such as Table 5.16 or they could even be broken down into more granular actions. The main advantages of Case Studies 7 and 8 are root cause analysis and saving time for the necessary actions for troubleshooting. Although applying supervised learning requires any kind of data annotation, the failure patterns for the failed test cases might be identified automatically via employing natural language processing techniques. Even when data labeling is performed manually, this will be a one time task, the results of which can be reused several times during the testing process.

5.6. Implementation

In this section, we will review some of the available methods for implementing test artifact vectorization in Python. We chose Python as our primary programming language because it is taught at a wide range of institutions, and at the time of writing this book, it is the most common language in the domain of exploratory data science. While this section is not going to provide a complete introduction to the language, it will focus on the supporting libraries and some concepts that we use to implement the examples in this book.

On its own, Python is an interpreted programming language without any specific features aimed at data science. The potential of using Python for data science lies in the rich ecosystem of libraries that can be used together to enable fast and accessible operations on large quantities of data. In the following subsections, we introduce the reader to the libraries (Section 5.6.1), then we will describe implementation approaches for vectorization of each type of the test artifacts (Sections 5.6.2–5.6.4) and handling of imbalanced data (Section 5.6.5), and finally we will discuss methods for data presentation (Section 5.6.6).

5.6.1 Scripts, modules, packages, and libraries

In the following subsections, we provide brief overviews of the most important libraries that are used in the examples in this book. As these libraries are constantly being updated, we advise the reader to always refer to the documentation for the versions of the libraries that they are using.

5.6.1.1 NumPy

```
import numpy as np

my_array = np.array([1, 2, 3, 4])

print(my_array.sum())
# Output: 10

print(my_array.dtype)
# Output: int64
```

Listing 5.1: A short NumPy program.

In Python, operations on vast amounts of numerical data can be exceedingly slow due to the large amount of type checking that occurs while executing Python programs [8]. The Python community overcame this issue by creating optimized libraries for common operations on vectors and matrices. NumPy is the most often utilized library that supports fast operations on multidimensional arrays and matrices. A sample of the code utilizing NumPy is presented in Listing 5.1. In this example, we create a

NumPy array with four elements and then print the sum of the elements of the array and the type of the elements of the array. Note that the array was created from a Python list where each element may be of a different type, but after conversion to a NumPy array, all elements are int64, thus enabling fast operations. In this example, we compute the sum of the elements within the array by calling the sum method of the my_array object. The output of the print statement is presented below it as a Python comment.

5.6.1.2 Pandas

```
import pandas as pd

df = pd.DataFrame(columns=['a','b','c'], data=[ [1, 2, 3], [10, 20, 30] ])

print(df.head())
# Output:
#      a   b   c
# 0    1   2   3
# 1   10  20  30

print(df.dtypes)
# Output:
# a      int64
# b      int64
# c      int64
# dtype: object

print(df.sum())
# Output:
# a    11
# b    22
# c    33
# dtype: int64
```

Listing 5.2: A short Pandas program.

While NumPy is primarily designed to hold and operate on an array or matrix of the same data type, Pandas is intended for operations on DataFrames, tables of data that can at the same time contain columns with various data types. In the example in Listing 5.2, we create a Pandas DataFrame df with three columns and two rows. Then we print the sums of each column. As our data could be described by using int64 type, the columns have that type, as well as the sums of the columns. The results are stored in a one-dimensional list that Pandas calls Series. Besides the baseline functionality for operations on DataFrames, Pandas provides interfaces for loading and saving data that support a variety of formats.

5.6.1.3 SentenceTransformer

```
from sentence_transformers import SentenceTransformer
model = SentenceTransformer('stsb-mpnet-base-v2')

# Define sentences for encoding
sentences = ['Set the both Return Air Damper Position as Closed for all HVACs
        across the train.',
    'Set the HVAC mode of Operation to Normal Mode',
    'The quick brown fox jumps over the lazy dog.']

#Sentences are encoded by calling model.encode()
embeddings = model.encode(sentences)

#Print the embeddings
for sentence, embedding in zip(sentences, embeddings):
    print("Sentence:", sentence)
    print("Embedding:", embedding)
    print("")

# Print the cosine similarity matrix
from sklearn.metrics.pairwise import cosine_similarity
print(cosine_similarity(embeddings))
# Output:
# [[1.0000001  0.5349122  0.06528943]
#  [0.5349122  1.0000001  0.09976764]
#  [0.06528943 0.09976764 0.9999998 ]]
```

Listing 5.3: SentenceTransformer example.

In this book, as the primary vectorization library for natural language representations of the text, we employ the SentenceTransformer library. This library is paired with a pre-trained model, stsb-mpnet-base-v2 [9], which is the best-rated model in the currently available official models published by the maintainers of SentenceTransformer.

In the example of SentenceTransformer, presented in Listing 5.3, we encode three sentences. Two of the encoded sentences are examples of content from the test scripts and the third one is the standard English-language pangram. After calculating the cosine similarity between the resulting embedding vectors, we can see that the two sentences are much more similar to each other than to the third one.

5.6.1.4 HDBSCAN

```
 1  import hdbscan
 2
 3  dataPoints = [ [0, 0, 0],
 4                 [5, 5, 5],
 5                 [0, 0, 0.1],
 6                 [0, 0.1, 0],
 7                 [0.1, 0, 0]]
 8
 9  clusterer = hdbscan.HDBSCAN(min_cluster_size=2, allow_single_cluster=True)
10
11  clusterer.fit(dataPoints)
12
13  print(clusterer.labels_)
14  # Output:
15  # [ 0 -1  0  0  0]
```

Listing 5.4: SentenceTransformer example.

After we have produced high-dimensional embedding vectors, we often want to identify which ones are clumped together. To achieve this, in this book we are utilizing the HDBSCAN algorithm, which is packaged in the Python library of the same name.

In Listing 5.4 we see a rudimentary example of usage of HDBSCAN. After importing hdbscan, we define five data points of which four are around the origin. Furthermore, we create an instance of the HDBSCAN cluster and modify it such that it can support very small clusters and output a single cluster. After clustering the data points we get the correct result. The settings of HDBSCAN can drastically change its behavior and create very different outputs. Thus it is important to understand the structure of the data and correctly select the parameters.

5.6.1.5 UMAP

In order to visualize the vector embeddings on a page, we need to represent the high-dimensional vectors using two or three dimensions. There are several algorithms that could be used for this purpose with primary candidates being t-SNE [10] and UMAP [11]. In Listing 5.5 we show a brief listing of the code that implements UMAP to dimensionally reduce the dataset from

```
 1  import umap
 2
 3  # %%
 4  dataPoints = [ [0, 0, 0], [5, 5, 5], [0, 0, 0.1], [0, 0.1, 0], [0.1, 0, 0]]
 5  # %%
 6  embedding = umap.UMAP(n_neighbors=2,
 7                        disconnection_distance=100,
 8                        min_dist=0.3,
 9                        metric='correlation').fit_transform(dataPoints)
10
11
12  # %%
13  print(embedding)
14  # Output:
15  # [[ 1.3283874  13.501315  ]
16  #  [ 0.33848003 13.790039  ]
17  #  [-0.73135513 12.274026  ]
18  #  [ 0.903116   12.705131  ]
19  #  [-2.6210678  10.203386  ]]
```

Listing 5.5: SentenceTransformer example.

three to two dimensions. Some parameters of the UMAP library have been
chosen to overcome the issues of using the trivial dataset.

5.6.1.6 AutoKeras

```
 1  import autokeras as ak
 2  clf = ak.StructuredDataClassifier(
 3      overwrite=True, max_trials=10
 4  )
 5
 6  clf.fit(x=X_train.astype(float), y=y_train.astype(int))
 7  y_pred = clf.predict(X_test) #classification
 8
 9  from sklearn.metrics import classification_report
10  print(classification_report(y_test, y_pred.astype(int)))
```

Listing 5.6: AutoKeras example.

AutoKeras is an open-source library for performing automated machine
learning for deep learning models. Various models are implemented using
the machine learning API called Keras that uses Tensorflow as the backend.
It provides a simple and effective approach for automatically finding ex-

cellent models for classifiers and regressors for images, text, and structured data.

The advantage of using automated machine learning tools is that it is highly applicable when the situation calls for the application of machine learning tools to a dataset with values that are not known to the data scientist but still carry meaning. This is often the case when vectorization methods described in this book are used. The resulting vector values do not have immediate interpretations but they still carry the abstract meaning of relationship to other entries in the dataset. Thus by applying automated machine learning techniques, we can automate the process of discovering the best-performing model for the current vectorization method and parameters such as the number of dimensions.

In Listing 5.6 we show the minimal implementation for using this method based on StructuredDataClassifier. We assume that the environment already contains traditionally named X_train, y_train, X_test, and y_test, corresponding to the training and testing datasets with their corresponding labels. AutoKeras will then during the training phase try max_trials=10 different models to fit the dataset and choose the best.

5.6.2 Text vectorization

In order to implement text vectorization, we are relying on SentenceTransformer and loading data using Pandas. An example of text vectorization is presented in Listing 5.7. Similar code to this was used to generate vectors for Case Studies 1 and 2.

```
import pandas as pd
import numpy as np
from hdbscan import HDBSCAN
from sentence_transformers import SentenceTransformer

testCases = pd.read_pickle("TestCases.pkl")

embeddings = (SentenceTransformer('stsb-mpnet-base-v2')
              .encode(testCases["text"]))

labels = (HDBSCAN()
          .fit(embeddings)
          .labels_)
```

Listing 5.7: Example of transforming text to vector embeddings and clustering.

First, we import all of the necessary libraries. Then we load the data into a Pandas data frame. For this, we use a Python standard approach to serialization of memory objects for disk storage called pickle, which is available in the library of the same name. We can either create a SentenceTransformer object from the given pre-trained model or create and immediately use this object. As we are not reusing the SentenceTransformer object and later the HDBSCAN object, we chain operations [12] to improve clarity and avoid keeping excessive variables.

As the aforementioned SentenceTransformer model outputs 768 dimensions, this step results in an $n_{TestCases} \times 768$ matrix stored in the embeddings variable. To group the test cases by similarity, we run HDBSCAN on the embedding vectors. HDBSCAN will try to identify the structure of the documents in space and find those that are close by. However, by default, HDBSCAN utilizes Euclidean distance as: $d(a, b) = d(b, a) = \sqrt{\sum_{i=1}^{n_{dim}} (b_i - a_i)^2}$, where n_{dim} is the number of dimensions and a_i and b_i are the values of the ith dimension of embedding vectors a and b. This distance is not always the optimal distance to use with word and document embeddings. An alternative distance, used in most literature, is the cosine distance. To use the cosine distance with HDBSCAN, we have three options shown in Listing 5.8.

```
# First approach
from sklearn.preprocessing import normalize

labels = (HDBSCAN()
          .fit(normalize(embeddings, norm='l2'))
          .labels_)


# Second approach
labels = (HDBSCAN(metric="cosine", algorithm="generic")
          .fit(embeddings)
          .labels_)


# Third approach
from sklearn.metrics.pairwise import pairwise_distances
labels = (HDBSCAN(metric='precomputed')
          .fit(pairwise_distances(embeddings, metric='cosine')
          .astype('float64'))
          .labels_)
```

Listing 5.8: Three approaches for using cosine distance with HDBSCAN.

In the first approach, we replace the cosine distance with the Euclidean distance of the L2 normalized dataset. Even though the two measures do not produce the same results, they will not influence the results of ranking or HDBSCAN. In the second approach, we change the algorithm used by HDBSCAN from the default `best` to `generic`. By doing this, we enable clustering using the built-in cosine distance; however, this will not work well for very large datasets.

In the third approach, we pre-compute all distances and then use the pre-computed metric of HDBSCAN. Due to incompatibility between packages, we need to convert the resulting pairwise distances into another data type.

5.6.3 Code vectorization

In order to achieve vectorization of test scripts, another approach is necessary. Our approach relies on Code2Vec [6], which represents code segments as embedding vectors. Code2Vec achieves this by decomposing the code into a number of paths represented by their abstract syntax tree. Then a neural network learns the aggregate structures of these path representations and from this neural network, embedding vectors are generated. This approach was used in Case Studies 5 and 6.

As the implementation of the Code2Vec depends on a large amount of pre-processing of source code, the simplest method to invoke it is to use the commands supplied with the original paper. After running training the model, each source file in the dataset will be accompanied by a `.vec` file containing embedding vectors for every function present in the original file. These files can then be loaded into a data frame with unique descriptors derived from the file title and the function name associated with each vector. From this point, the data can be clustered in the same manner as the text in the previous section.

5.6.4 Log vectorization

For vectorization of logs, we use the Log2Vec implementation [13] from the original paper that introduces the method. The advantage of the Log2Vec approach is that it supports out-of-vocabulary word learning at runtime.

To vectorize the logs in Case Studies 7 and 8, we have used the command provided in Listing 5.9 with the logs provided in the input file `TestingLogs.log` with each log contained in a single row.

```
python pipeline.py -i data/TestingLogs.log -t TestingLogs -o results/
```

Listing 5.9: Example of Log2Vec execution.

After running the code, the output can be found in the `TestingLogs` subfolder of the `results` folder. We are interested in the file `log.vector` that contains embedding vectors for the input logs. From here we can proceed with clustering and similarity tests as in the previous section.

5.6.5 Random over-sampling, under-sampling, and SMOTE

When the dataset that we use for training or evaluation is heavily imbalanced with a representation of one label significantly different from other labels, we can introduce some method of over-sampling, under-sampling, or the synthetic minority over-sampling technique (SMOTE) to correct it. If there are enough samples in the under-represented label, we can apply under-sampling to the over-represented samples. If the number of samples is too low to under-sample, we can try to over-sample the under-represented label. Last, when the interpolation between samples is possible and valid, we can apply SMOTE to add synthetic samples to fill up the under-represented labels.

The provided Python code in Listing 5.10 can be employed for performing the under-sampling approach for solving the binary classification problem for dependent and independent test cases. In this case, we have used a custom implementation of the under-sampling algorithm to address the problem of measuring whether any two of the test cases are in the same cluster in the ground truth as in the clustered dataset.

The provided Python code in Listing 5.11 can be employed for performing the over-sampling approach for solving a general classification problem.

The provided Python code in Listing 5.12 can be employed for implementing the presented combined approach for solving a general classification problem. This approach can be very efficient in situations where there are multiple labels with some labels that need over-sampling and some that need under-sampling.

Another approach to constructing a balanced dataset is to add synthetic samples. One algorithm for this is called SMOTE [14] and a simple application of it is presented in Listing 5.13. To generate the code we used the function `make_classification`, which can generate datasets of various shapes and labels. The generated dataset is presented in Fig. 5.18

```
1  # links is a dictionary representing the ground truth
2  # in the format links['tc1'] = set('tc2', 'tc3')
3  # labels is a dictionary with the result of clustering
4  # in the format labels['tc1'] = n
5  # where n>=-1 is an integer with -1 being unclustered
6
7  from random import random
8
9  n_0 = 0
10 n_1 = 0
11 for a,b in combinations(links.keys(), 2):
12     if (b in links[a]) or (a in links[b]):
13         n_1 += 1
14     else:
15         n_0 +=1
16
17 tp = 0 # True Positive
18 fp = 0 # False Positive
19 tn = 0 # True Negative
20 fn = 0 # False Negative
21 for a,b in combinations(links.keys(), 2):
22     ground_truth = (b in links[a]) or (a in links[b])
23     if (not ground_truth) and (random() >= (n_1 / n_0)):
24         continue
25     if labels[a] == -1 and labels[b] == -1:
26         if ground_truth:
27             fn += 1
28         else:
29             tn += 1
30     elif labels[a] == labels[b]:
31         if ground_truth:
32             tp += 1
33         else:
34             fp += 1
35     else:
36         if ground_truth:
37             fn += 1
38         else:
39             tn += 1
40 print("With subsampling:")
41 print("TP\tFP\tTN\tFN")
42 print("{}\t{}\t{}\t{}".format(tp,fp,tn,fn))
```

Listing 5.10: Python source code for under-sampling the dataset to correct pairwise comparison imbalance.

```
from imblearn.over_sampling import RandomOverSampler
ros = RandomOverSampler()
X_train_resampled, y_train_resampled = ros.fit_resample(X_train, y_train)
```

Listing 5.11: Source code for over-sampling the dataset to create a balanced dataset for learning algorithms.

```
from imblearn.over_sampling import RandomOverSampler
from imblearn.under_sampling import RandomUnderSampler
over = RandomOverSampler(sampling_strategy=0.1)
X_train, y_train = over.fit_resample(X_train, y_train)
under = RandomUnderSampler(sampling_strategy=0.5)
X_train, y_train = under.fit_resample(X_train, y_train)
```

Listing 5.12: Source code for combined under- and over-sampling the dataset to create a balanced dataset for learning algorithms.

```
from collections import Counter
from numpy import size
from sklearn.datasets import make_classification
from imblearn.over_sampling import SMOTE
X, y = make_classification(n_classes=2, class_sep=2,
weights=[0.1, 0.9], n_informative=2, n_redundant=0, flip_y=0,
n_features=2, n_clusters_per_class=1, n_samples=100, random_state=42)
print('Original dataset label ratio {}'.format(Counter(y)))
# Original dataset label ratio Counter({1: 90, 0: 10})

sm = SMOTE(random_state=42)
X_res, y_res = sm.fit_resample(X, y)
print('Resampled dataset label ratio {}'.format(Counter(y_res)))
# Resampled dataset label ratio Counter({1: 90, 0: 90})
```

Listing 5.13: Source code for SMOTE over-sampling the dataset to create a balanced dataset with synthetic samples.

alongside the resampled dataset. As can be seen from the code listing and Fig. 5.18, SMOTE generated new data points within the region of the under-represented label.

5.6.6 Visualization implementation

In order to visualize the results of the embedding, we need to reduce dimensionality. In the case of our SentenceTransformer example, we need to reduce the dimensionality from 768 to three or two dimensions. A way to

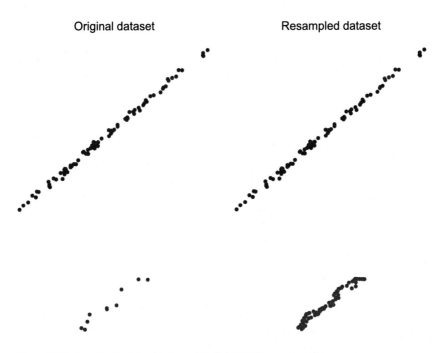

Figure 5.18 A synthetic dataset before and after SMOTE over-sampling.

do this is to use the UMAP algorithm. In Listing 5.14 we show an example of the use of UMAP and simple visualization.

```
from umap import UMAP
import matplotlib.pyplot as plt
import seaborn as sns

coordinates = UMAP().fit_transform(embeddings)

sns.set()
plt.scatter(x = coordinates[:, 0], y = coordinates[:, 1], c = labels)
plt.show()
```

Listing 5.14: Example of reducing dimensionality of vector embeddings using UMAP and plotting them on a scatter plot.

As in previous sections, since we are not going to be reusing the UMAP object, we create an object and immediately apply it to transform the embedding vectors. By default, this UMAP implementation maps the input to two dimensions. Then we use the seaborn package to style the graphs output by `matplotlib` and create a simple scatterplot. It is worth noting that while the relative positions between the embeddings represent distances, the actual values of dimensionally reduced vectors are rarely useful.

References

[1] P. Baxter, S. Jack, Qualitative case study methodology: Study design and implementation for novice researchers, The Qualitative Report 13 (2008) 544–559.

[2] P. Runeson, M. Höst, Guidelines for conducting and reporting case study research in software engineering, Empirical Software Engineering 14 (2) (2009) 131–164.

[3] S. Tahvili, Multi-criteria optimization of system integration testing, PhD thesis, Malardalen University, December 2018.

[4] Z. Jin, Chapter 2 – requirements engineering methodologies, in: Z. Jin (Ed.), Environment Modeling-Based Requirements Engineering for Software Intensive Systems, Morgan Kaufmann, Oxford, 2018, pp. 13–27.

[5] S. Tahvili, M. Bohlin, M. Saadatmand, S. Larsson, W. Afzal, D. Sundmark, Cost-benefit analysis of using dependency knowledge at integration testing, in: Product-Focused Software Process Improvement, Springer International Publishing, 2016, pp. 268–284.

[6] U. Alon, M. Zilberstein, O. Levy, E. Yahav, Code2Vec: Learning distributed representations of code, Proceedings of the ACM on Programming Languages 3 (POPL) (2019) 40:1–40:29.

[7] M. Friendly, Mosaic displays for multi-way contingency tables, Journal of the American Statistical Association 89 (425) (1994) 190–200.

[8] F. Cady, The Data Science Handbook, Wiley, 2017.

[9] N. Reimers, I. Gurevych Sentence-bert, Sentence embeddings using Siamese BERT-networks, in: Proceedings of the 2019 Conference on Empirical Methods in Natural Language Processing, Association for Computational Linguistics, 2019.

[10] Y. Kim, D. Kim, A. Kumar, R. Sarikaya, Efficient large-scale neural domain classification with personalized attention, in: Proceedings of the 56th Annual Meeting of the Association for Computational Linguistics (Volume 1: Long Papers), 2018, pp. 2214–2224.

[11] L. McInnes, J. Healy, J. Melville, UMAP: Uniform manifold approximation and projection for dimension reduction, arXiv preprint, arXiv:1802.03426, 2018.

[12] M. Harrison, T. Petrou, Pandas 1.x Cookbook: Practical Recipes for Scientific Computing, Time Series Analysis and Exploratory Data Analysis Using Python, 2020, oCLC: 1147864211.

[13] W. Meng, Y. Liu, Y. Huang, S. Zhang, F. Zaiter, B. Chen, D. Pei, A semantic-aware representation framework for online log analysis, in: 2020 29th International Conference on Computer Communications and Networks (ICCCN), IEEE, 2020, pp. 1–7.

[14] N. Chawla, K. Bowyer, L. Hall, W. Kegelmeyer, Smote: Synthetic minority oversampling technique, Journal of Artificial Intelligence Research 16 (2002) 321–357.

CHAPTER SIX

Benefits, results, and challenges of artificial intelligence

Chapter points

- This chapter provides some barriers and challenges to implementing artificial intelligence in the industry.
- We present an outlook of the economic benefits of employing artificial intelligence in industries.
- We provide an artificial intelligence platform pipeline.
- We discuss the required cost for implementing artificial intelligence from scratch in the industry.

"Anything that could give rise to smarter-than-human intelligence – in the form of Artificial Intelligence, brain–computer interfaces, or neuroscience-based human intelligence enhancement – wins hands down beyond contest as doing the most to change the world. Nothing else is even in the same league."

Eliezer Yudkowsky

6.1. Benefits and barriers to the adoption of artificial intelligence

During the last decade, employing artificial intelligence has proven its worth with a great potential to carry enterprises to become more intelligent, productive, and also more competitive. According to Gartner's special report [1], the employment of artificial intelligence in businesses has increased by up to 270% between 2015 and 2019. The main increase is observed in the high information technology industry and also telecommunications companies for automating workflows, processes, and decision-making. On the other hand, 88% of the participants in the 2020/21 World Quality Report emphasized that artificial intelligence is the strongest growth area of their test activities [2].

In this regard, the conducted studies on applying artificial intelligence in software development show that converting natural language instructions into machine-readable data has received a great deal of attention since

Artificial Intelligence Methods for Optimization of the Software Testing Process
https://doi.org/10.1016/B978-0-32-391913-5.00017-8

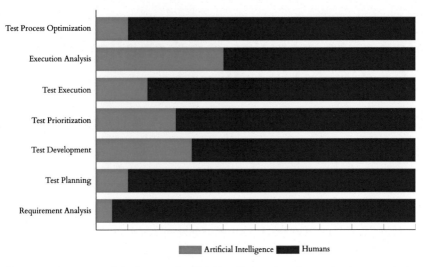

Figure 6.1 A segment of the impact of artificial intelligence in software development during 2020–2021. Sources: World Quality Report [2] and Gartner's special report [1].

2020. As already presented in this book, most of the test artifacts are still created by humans and they follow human-readable rules. Therefore, artificial intelligence has found opportunities to improve human work in the testing domain. Analyzing the artificial intelligence movement in the past few years, we can see how the effort in software development today will be impacted by artificial intelligence in the near future. Fig. 6.1 indicates some of the potential spots. The blue bars show manual effort is expended in the software development life cycle today, and the green bars represented where artificial intelligence had an impact in 2020–2021.

As we can see in Fig. 6.1, the utilization of artificial intelligence for test execution analysis has increased more compared to all other phases in the software development life cycle. As we highlighted in the provided case studies, analyzing the test artifacts can help the testing team to establish the basis of test cases. In this regard, applying different artificial intelligence technologies and especially natural language processing shows great potential in the testing domain. According to Gartner's report, today's artificial intelligence technologies for software development have the potential to combine with scripted automation techniques to automate up to 70% of the current manual work by the testing team [1]. This statement is also highlighted in the 2020/2021 World Quality Report as the "Test Development" in Fig. 6.1. During 2021, the employment of artificial intelligence technologies for test automation purposes increased by up to 26% at the unit testing level and by 23.5% at the integration and acceptance testing levels [1].

Combining the topics of "Test Prioritization" and "Process Optimization" in Fig. 6.1 also indicates the ability of the artificial intelligence technologies for improving the testing process in terms of time and cost reduction. As presented in the industrial case studies, test optimization in terms of test case selection, prioritization, and minimization are the main applications of the proposed artificial intelligence-based solutions in this book.

Assessing the presented reports, a huge gap in artificial intelligence involvement in software development can be observed. Even though most companies aim to deploy artificial intelligence, many are at an early stage of this process.

But what is the barrier to the widespread adoption of artificial intelligence in the industry?

While this might seem like a simple question, the answer can be complex. As with all other presented problems and solutions in this book, getting past artificial intelligence's barriers to entry is a multi-criterion problem.

Back in 2018, Gartner made a widely shared prediction that through 2022, up to 85% of artificial intelligence projects would deliver erroneous outcomes due to bias in data, algorithms, or the teams responsible for managing them [3]. However, due to paying no attention to the artificial intelligence challenges, the predicted failure rate has remained, and most industry leaders have continued to make similar predictions. The McKinsey Institute Global Survey on artificial intelligence indicated that in 2021, only 21% of respondents claimed they had rolled out artificial intelligence in more than one process [4].

Fig. 6.2 presents some of the barriers and challenges for artificial intelligence adoption in industries. Although the barriers of artificial intelligence might be more than the pointed factors in Fig. 6.2, we aimed to summarize those challenges that we faced during our research. In summary, *choosing a poor architecture, training data availability and quality, lack of artificial intelligence explainability*, and *ongoing fees* can be considered as the main challenges that the enterprises need to tackle. However, many of the barriers in Fig. 6.2 especially from a cost perspective are avoidable with a little common-sense business thinking and top management support [5].

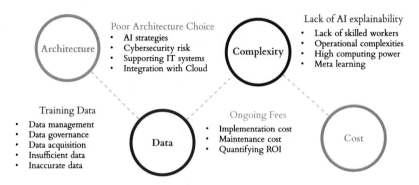

Figure 6.2 Some of the common artificial intelligence challenges. Source: Author's own contributions.

In the upcoming section, we exemplify the mentioned barriers in an industrial context, and we provide some practical solutions for them.

6.2. Artificial intelligence platform pipeline

A workflow in artificial intelligence considers several steps to prepare and analyze data, train and evaluate models, and deploy trained models to production. Providing an artificial intelligence platform where enterprises can orchestrate the mentioned steps in the workflow as a pipeline can be considered a practical solution for artificial intelligence adoption in industries. In this regard, Gartner coined AIOps in 2016, which stands for *Artificial Intelligence for IT Operations*. AIOps is the umbrella term for machine learning analytics technology which aims to facilitate automate, manage, and audit machine learning workflows [6]. Another useful concept that needs to be considered for utilizing machine learning approaches in industries is MLOps [7]. In summary, MLOps is a combination of the continuous development practice of DevOps and data engineering, which aims to deploy and maintain machine learning systems in production reliably and efficiently. According to a published report by Gartner in 2020, MLOps is a powerful framework that can be applied to successfully operationalize machine learning projects in the industry [8].

However, there are many ways to introduce a new artificial intelligence system into the production pipeline. Some of the simplest approaches can be by interfacing an Automated Machine Learning (AutoML) system to a database that is already part of the production process. In order to get

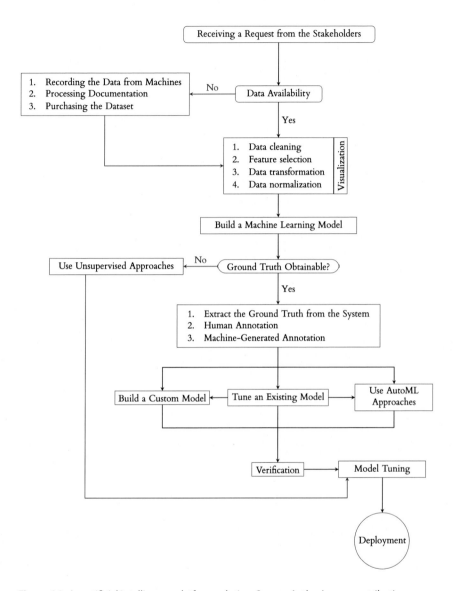

Figure 6.3 An artificial intelligence platform solution. Source: Author's own contributions.

effective results, often significantly more steps are necessary. In Fig. 6.3 we present an overview of the typical artificial intelligence application process. We will look at the process across three phases: dataset generation, model development, and model deployment.

6.2.1 Dataset generation

The first step toward artificial intelligence is to define a dataset and obtain it. Often datasets are available as side products of the production process, such as a variety of logs, software repositories, or spreadsheets tracking a variety of variables. However, it is a common case that the data necessary for successful artificial intelligence development is not immediately available. In such cases we have three general approaches to data–gathering:

- **Recording the data from machines.** This is the approach where the data is already generated by machines but is currently not recorded. In this case, instrumenting the machines with the recording equipment can result in extraordinary quantities of data. If we are considering physical production machines, a common way to achieve instrumentation is to add instrumentation using OPC-UA[1] protocols. In other cases, we can consider a variety of servers and applications as machines. Then the instrumentation has to be adjusted to the previously existing infrastructure.

- **Processing documentation.** This refers to processing documentation such as procedures, service manuals, or legacy bookkeeping into machine-readable formats. This approach can be semi-automated but this can also introduce very large amounts of noise into data. For example, if we are processing printed documents, a problem in the printer can introduce repeated errors in the dataset by consistently introducing errors in OCR[2] process of the text present on those pages.

- **Purchasing the dataset**. This can be a very efficient approach. As the popularity of artificial intelligence is growing, the number of companies that are offering their cleaned-up and labeled datasets for purchase is growing rapidly. The availability of datasets varies by industry and the necessary quality and volume of data.

After the data has been obtained from external or internal sources, every dataset has to be adjusted to the needs of the specific system. There are several stages to this process. It is very important to make sure that this process is repeatable and well documented, as the dataset often needs to be readjusted and additional errors in the dataset may be identified at any stage of the model development process. There are four types of data processing that need to be done on the dataset to prepare it for machine learning:

---

[1] OPC–UA or OPC Unified Architecture is a cross-platform, open-source IEC62541 standard for data exchange developed by the OPC Foundation.

[2] Optical Character Recognition (OCR) is a set of technologies for automated conversion of scanned documents into a computer-readable format.

- **Data cleaning**. Data cleaning is almost always necessary. In this step, the invalid data is removed. This can be missing data entries that need to be filled in with default values or the removal of values that are outside of the valid range. For example, let us take the room temperature recorded by the sensor. Some values might be simply missing and thus result in 0 after conversion or a faulty sensor can result in ∞ temperature. These types of irregularities would have very bad effects on the machine learning algorithm and thus have to be either replaced or removed from the dataset.

- **Feature selection.** Feature selection is a process of selecting which recorded features should be included in the model. We can guide the training of a machine learning model by selecting the input variables that are relevant to the output variables. By carefully selecting features, we can also work towards reducing undesirable biases that are being introduced into the model.

- **Data transformation.** Data transformation or feature extraction is a process that transforms existing features into forms that are more suitable for machine learning. A number of features that are obvious to human readers are not formatted in ways that suit machine learning models. For example, if the dataset has dates, useful features that can be extracted from it are whether the day is working or non-working, or, in the case of sales, how far the date is from the previous common salary day. Furthermore, text data needs to be converted into useful formats, as was already discussed in the previous chapters of this book.

- **Data normalization.** Data normalization is an application of various normalization approaches to scale the values into common ranges. For artificial intelligence applications, it is often better to scale values of various measurements to the range of [0, 1] or [−1, 1] instead of having the specific values. During this step, we can also convert various units into mutually comparable quantities.

After we have the initial dataset, we need to consider whether it has data labels included in the dataset or the data needs to be labeled. In the case that the data cannot be labeled, we can still apply a variety of unsupervised learning approaches to the dataset such as clustering, dimensionality reduction approaches, or autoencoder neural networks, and more. For adding the labels we have three major approaches:

- **Ground truth from the system.** The ground truth from the system can be extracted when the results are already known and logged in the system. For example, if we have a large quantity of data describing the quality of the sub-components as well as quality control results on the finished products, we can build a strong dataset that can help us discover combinations of problems in sub-components that result in bad final products.

- **Human annotation.** Human annotation is one of the most common approaches to annotating datasets with labels. Besides having clear instructions, it is also important to have more than one expert working on the labeling process and experts need to label some of the same rows of data. Otherwise, there is a risk of the introduction of undetectable biases or conflicted labeling.

- **Machine-generated annotation.** Machine-generated annotation can be employed in some cases. One of the most common times to employ it is when the dataset is also machine-generated and thus the labels are known a priori. A more general approach can be when used in conjunction with human annotation. In many cases, support software for assisting humans in labeling can be used to reduce the total cost of this process [9].

6.2.2 Model development

There are three major options for the development of a machine learning model from a dataset and ground truth. The least involved approach is to use *AutoML approaches*. A number of platforms provide AutoML services that will try several generic models and find and tune one that fits the best to the dataset. While it provides an effective initial state of the model, for critical systems it is useful to *build a custom model* as it gives more insight into the inner workings of the model. Several use cases have been already addressed by researchers and their models are freely reusable in industrial settings. In such cases, it can be beneficial to *fine-tune an existing model*. Moreover, leveraging a pre-trained machine learning model has other substantial benefits, e.g., it is very simple to incorporate, it has a quick performance, and there is not as much labeled data required.

6.2.3 Model deployment

Once the initial model has been trained, it is necessary to verify its performance and detect any unwanted biases. This can be done by introducing noise into the initial dataset and verifying against this new noisy dataset or by capturing new data and using it to verify the quality of the model. If there are problems detected in the model, it is often necessary to go back to the initial data pre-processing steps and further refine the initial dataset.

Once the model is performing satisfactorily, it can be deployed. The type of deployment depends on the amount of data that needs to be processed, the time in which it needs to be processed, and the devices that are available for it. In general, artificial intelligence models are often deployed on a cloud infrastructure, many of which have specialized support for artificial intelligence models. These deployments are good for processing large quantities of data while maintaining controlled costs. On the opposite end of the deployment spectrum lie embedded machine learning models, where the resources are at a premium, so it is necessary to distinguish between models that need to be trained on the device and models that will be just used for inference.

When deploying machine learning models, the cybersecurity of the model is an important factor to consider. As the popularity of artificial intelligence models is growing, so do the available attacks against them. Today, several security threats against artificial intelligence applications and also machine learning models are identified, e.g., data privacy, transfer learning attacks, and online system manipulation [10]. Furthermore, it is now possible to extract the model without the direct ability to read the model [11]. Thus industrial-grade solutions such as hardware security modules need to be used in conjunction with a well-designed architecture.

6.3. Costs of artificial intelligence integration into the software development life cycle

"What are the true costs of implementing artificial intelligence" is one of the first questions that we received from the stakeholders during this research. Although the simple answer is "it depends," in reality, many enterprises cannot afford the implementation costs of artificial intelligence.

But what makes artificial intelligence expensive?

The artificial intelligence model's complexity, performance requirements, and subsequently costs vary greatly. However, there are several factors that affect the real cost of developing artificial intelligence, and we are going to examine some of those factors in this section.

- *The level of intelligence.* In order to differentiate the level of intelligence in different types of artificial intelligence machines, extensive research has been performed. The conducted research indicates that artificial intelligence can be categorized mainly into Strong Artificial Intelligence and also Weak Artificial Intelligence [12]. This categorization can also be divided into the following main classes based on the capabilities:

1. *Artificial narrow intelligence.* Artificial narrow intelligence (ANI) can be considered as the most common, available type of artificial intelligence. An ANI is an intelligence system that is designed to solve just a single, specific task. ANIs generally have a narrow capability and they show good performance for instance for weather prediction [13].

2. *Artificial general intelligence.* Artificial general intelligence (AGI) aims to be a machine capable of understanding the world and human behaviors. AGI is designed to learn how to carry out a huge range of different tasks. Although most research emphasizes that AGI is still at a nascent stage, the capabilities of AGI systems could be boosted to a level beyond human abilities [13,14]. There are two general approaches to developing AGI: (1) computer science-oriented and (2) neuroscience-oriented. Moreover, hypothesis testing, analogy, and recognition can be mentioned as other properties of AGI systems.

3. *Artificial super intelligence.* Artificial super intelligence (ASI) represents the future of artificial intelligence. Currently, it can be considered as a hypothetical concept that assumes a surpassing of human intelligence [15]. In theory, ASI machines will be able to perform extraordinary things that only humans are capable of today, such as decision-making and even art [16].

Although all of the mentioned intelligence levels are not achievable today, most business artificial intelligence solutions can be described as ANI.

• *The amount and quality of data.* As we have already shown in the conducted case studies in this book, the performance of an artificial intelligence-based solution is directly related to the quality of the data. By data quality, we mean data consistency, integrity, accuracy, size, and completeness. Generally, the available data in the industry can be both structured data, stored in relational database management systems (e.g., the DOORS database), or unstructured data, e.g., Internet of Things and sensor data. However, working on unstructured data is more expensive due to the required extra steps to organize, clean, normalize, and also label it. Therefore, utilizing structured data, especially in large industries, it is cheaper to train the artificial intelligence algorithms. Data privacy and security such as General Data Protection Regulation (GDPR)[3] is another barrier that can increase the total cost of

---

[3] The General Data Protection Regulation 2016/679 is a regulation in EU law on data protection and privacy in the European Union.

implementing an artificial intelligence-based solution. Controlling the GDPR's principles for risk management and finding optimal solutions are challenging as well as costly tasks.

- *Artificial intelligence infrastructure.* The infrastructure includes almost every stage of a machine learning workflow to test, train, and deploy an artificial intelligence-based solution. The total cost behind the artificial intelligence infrastructure can be broken down into the price of a cluster of distributed GPUs[4] and computing power. When creating production software, additional costs need to be considered, such as a cloud-driven backend, extract–transform–load (ETL), API support, and other streaming tools and applications.

In summary, considering the above-mentioned factors can help enterprises to estimate the cost to develop an artificial intelligence-based solution. In 2019, the Forbes Technology Council [17] estimated that deploying an artificial intelligence-based solution will ultimately cost the enterprises up to 15 times more than the original plan. However, the attention for artificial intelligence deployment since 2020 helped enterprises to minimize the costs by starting small artificial intelligence projects.

References

[1] K. Costello, Gartner survey shows 37 percent of organizations have implemented AI in some form, http://www.gartner.com/en/newsroom/press-releases/2019-01-21-gartner-survey-shows-37-percent-of-organizations-have, 2019.

[2] Capgemini, World quality report 2020/21, http://www.capgemini.com/research/world-quality-report-wqr-20-21/, 2020. (Accessed January 2022).

[3] R. Meulen, T. McCall, Gartner says nearly half of CIOs are planning to deploy artificial intelligence, http://www.gartner.com/en/newsroom/press-releases/2018-02-13-gartner-says-nearly-half-of-cios-are-planning-to-deploy-artificial-intelligence, 2018.

[4] C. Michael Bryce, S. Alex, S. Alex, The state of AI in 2021, https://www.mckinsey.com/business-functions/mckinsey-analytics/our-insights/global-survey-the-state-of-ai-in-2021, 2021.

[5] J. Radhakrishnan, M. Chattopadhyay, Determinants and barriers of artificial intelligence adoption – a literature review, 2020, pp. 89–99.

[6] S. Shetty, Gartner says algorithmic it operations drives digital business, http://www.gartner.com/en/newsroom/press-releases/2017-04-11-gartner-says-algorithmic-it-operations-drives-digital-business, 2017.

[7] S. Alla, S.K. Adari, What Is MLOps?, Apress, Berkeley, CA, 2021, pp. 79–124.

[8] S. Vashisth, E. Brethenoux, F. Choudhary, J. Hare, Use Gartner's 3-stage MLOps framework to successfully operationalize machine learning projects, http://www.gartner.com/document/3987104, 2020.

[9] M. Desmond, E. Duesterwald, K. Brimijoin, M. Brachman, Q. Pan, Semi-automated data labeling, in: H.J. Escalante, K. Hofmann (Eds.), Proceedings of the NeurIPS 2020

---

[4] Graphics processing unit.

Competition and Demonstration Track, in: Proceedings of Machine Learning Research, vol. 133, 2021, pp. 156–169, https://proceedings.mlr.press/v133/desmond21a.html.

[10] Y. Hu, W. Kuang, Z. Qin, K. Li, J. Zhang, Y. Gao, W. Li, K. Li, Artificial intelligence security: Threats and countermeasures, ACM Computing Surveys 55 (1) (November 2021).

[11] N. Carlini, M. Jagielski, I. Mironov, Cryptanalytic extraction of neural network models, in: D. Micciancio, T. Ristenpart (Eds.), Advances in Cryptology – CRYPTO 2020, Springer International Publishing, Cham, 2020, pp. 189–218.

[12] E. Hildt, Artificial intelligence: Does consciousness matter?, Frontiers in Psychology 10 (2019).

[13] B. Goertzel, C. Pennachin, Artificial General Intelligence, Cognitive Technologies, Springer, Berlin, Heidelberg, 2010.

[14] J. Pei, L. Deng, S. Song, M. Zhao, Y. Zhang, S. Wu, G. Wang, Z. Zou, Z. Wu, W. He, F. Chen, N. Deng, S. Wu, Y. Wang, Y. Wu, Z. Yang, C. Ma, G. Li, W. Han, L. Shi, Towards artificial general intelligence with hybrid Tianjic chip architecture, Nature 572 (2019) 106.

[15] A.C. Neubauer, The future of intelligence research in the coming age of artificial intelligence – with a special consideration of the philosophical movements of trans- and posthumanism, Intelligence 87 (2021) 101563.

[16] K. Gill, Artificial super intelligence: beyond rhetoric, Artificial Intelligence and Society 31 (February 2016).

[17] S. Carrico, Good news: A successful AI project will cost 15 times more than you think, https://www.forbes.com/sites/forbestechcouncil/2019/07/02/good-news-a-successful-ai-project-will-cost-15-times-more-than-you-think/?sh=5be5c724474d, 2019.

## CHAPTER SEVEN

Discussion and concluding remarks

Chapter points

- This chapter provides a summary of the main contributions presented in this book.

"The key to artificial intelligence has always been the representation."

Jeff Hawkins

7.1. Closing remarks

The overall goal of this book is to provide some solutions for employing artificial intelligence techniques to improve the software testing process.

To work towards this goal, we have conducted research in three sequential stages: (1) identifying some potential improvement areas in the domain of manual integration testing, (2) applying several artificial intelligence techniques on the conducted data from two different domains of software testing, and (3) empirically evaluating the effectiveness of the proposed artificial intelligence-based solutions at industries. All included case studies in this book build on empirical research by performing several industrial case studies at Alstom Sweden AB and Ericsson AB.

The proposed artificial intelligence-based solutions in this book are not limited to software testing; they can be also adapted to other domains. However, the input data to the proposed pipelines in this book needs to be made computer-readable.

Manual test specifications written in a natural language format are a treasure trove of data that is often untapped in industrial environments. On the other hand, the natural language processing models are developing at breakneck speeds. Thus the newest natural language processing models might show better performance for analyzing a natural text. However, in the software testing domain, the prevalence of non-English tokens related to components of the tested product makes custom and customized language models a very valuable tool.

Artificial Intelligence Methods for Optimization of the Software Testing Process
https://doi.org/10.1016/B978-0-32-391913-5.00018-X

Today, there are various approaches to the vectorization of software testing artifacts. We need to consider that the best approach is dependent on the data type, pre-processing, and intended use of the artifacts.

Finally, relying fully on artificial intelligence for supporting and optimizing a testing process is still not a viable approach in the safety-critical domain. Therefore, the role of the software testing team is not going to disappear. In this book, we aimed to provide some artificial intelligence-based solutions which can be utilized as additional tools in the testing team's ever-expanding tool set.

## PART TWO

Practical examples and exercises

## CHAPTER EIGHT

Environment installation

Chapter points

- This chapter presents basic methods to install the environment necessary for the completion of the exercises in this book.

"When done well, software is invisible."

Bjarne Stroustrup

8.1. JupyterLab installation

As the primarily recommended environment for the execution of the exercises in this book, we recommend JupyterLab to any beginners. However, there is a variety of available environments available and the most widely used one or the one most compatible with the target industrial setting is usually the best choice.

JupyterLab is a free and open-source web-based environment for editing and running Jupyter Notebooks and other code, and serves as a terminal to interact with the operating system that the environment is running in. It allows users to configure and arrange workflows in data science, scientific computing, computational journalism, and machine learning. With a modular design, JupyterLab and Notebooks allow for extensions that enrich functionality such as creating slideshow presentations immediately from your Notebook (there is native functionality for this, and this can be extended one using the RISE[1] extension).

JupyterLab understands many other file formats (images, CSV, JSON, Markdown, PDF, Vega, Vega-Lite, etc.) and can also display rich output in these formats. Furthermore, Jupyter Notebooks can create interactive components that allow on-the-fly adjustment of parameters that are used in the workflow and thus enable the creation of interactive documents.

JupyterLab is served from the same server as Jupyter Notebook documents. Such server is usually running on the local machine or there

---

[1] RISE extensions for Jupyter Notebook slideshows can be found at https://rise.readthedocs.io/.

Artificial Intelligence Methods for Optimization of the Software Testing Process
https://doi.org/10.1016/B978-0-32-391913-5.00020-8

are centralized servers running multiple JupyterLab/Jupyter Notebook instances within a company environment.

The most straightforward approach to installing JupyterLab for macOS or Microsoft Windows is to use the Anaconda[2] installer and package manager. The Anaconda installer has the option to install most of the tools that are needed for data science pipelines, including Python and JupyterLab. Furthermore, packages mentioned in this book are available via Anaconda's package manager `conda`.

8.1.1 JupyterLab on pre-installed Python

While installing JupyterLab and Python together is useful in many situations, some developers already have Python installed on their machines and want to install only the JupyterLab servers. First, we need at least Python version 3.6 for most of the approaches used in this book. To ensure that you have the correct Python version, you can issue the command `python3 --version` from the terminal.

Python uses the concept of environments to specify which packages are available to an instance of Python interpreter. There is usually a global environment (commonly called `base` in conda) and a number of custom environments that are related to various projects one might have. Having multiple environments becomes the easiest way to solve conflicts between various packages. Package conflicts are most often created when multiple packages require the same package but in different versions.

JupyterLab can be installed using conda, mamba, or pip. To install JupyterLab globally, you can use one of these three commands depending on whether your Python package management is conducted using conda, mamba, or pip.[3]

- **conda:** conda install –c conda-forge jupyterlab
- **mamba:** mamba install –c conda-forge jupyterlab
- **pip:** pip3 install jupyterlab

After installation, you can start JupyterLab by issuing command `jupyter lab` on the command line.

Furthermore, you can install the entire system for JupyterLab in a Docker environment. If you have Docker installed, you can install and use

---

[2] Anaconda installers are available at https://www.anaconda.com/.

[3] Further up-to-date information about the environments can be found in our exercise repository at https://github.com/leohatvani/testing-optimization-exercises/.

JupyterLab by selecting one of the many ready-to-run Docker images maintained by the Jupyter Team. Ensure your docker command includes the `-e` `JUPYTER_ENABLE_LAB=yes` flag to ensure that JupyterLab is enabled.

8.2. GitHub labs

In this section, we provide a guideline for the reader on how to download and load the exercises into JupyterLab.

8.2.1 Download

The supporting source code and up-to-date instructions for the exercises in the book are available on GitHub. To download all the Labs, please go to GitHub (https://testing-optimization.com/exercises/) and click "Code → Download ZIP" to download the Zip file. After the download is completed, you must unzip this file before using the data from the exercises.

8.2.2 Loading the exercises into JupyterLab

To open the files with the templates for exercises in JupyterLab, first make sure that they are unzipped. Then, either make sure that the files are available within folders that JupyterLab can access or use the upload feature of JupyterLab to upload the files within the workspace.

## CHAPTER NINE

Exercises

Chapter points

- This chapter provides some essential exercises which can help Python users learn the necessary Python skills quickly.

"I love deadlines. I love the whooshing noise they make as they go by."

Douglas Adams, The Salmon of Doubt

9.1. Python exercises and practice

For a complete and practical understanding and the ability to apply the knowledge, both theoretical understanding and practice are needed [1]. The first three examples described in Chapter 5 have several components in common. For each, there is a set of variables that might be denoted as inputs, which are measured or pre-set. These have some influence on one or more outputs. For each example, the goal is to use the inputs to predict the values of the outputs. We have used the more modern language of machine learning. In the statistical literature the inputs are often called the predictors, a term we will use interchangeably with inputs, and more classically the independent variables. In the pattern recognition literature, the term features is preferred, which we use as well. The outputs are called the responses, or classically the dependent variables.

The exercises in this chapter are designed to help the readers develop their analysis skills by providing them with the opportunity to practice breaking down problems into sequences of steps. In addition, completing these exercises will help the readers to become further familiar with Python's syntax and the libraries typically used for machine learning and natural language processing. The exercises are further supported by data, notes, and outlines on the authors' website.[1]

---

[1] For more information about the exercises, visit https://testing-optimization.com/exercises.

Artificial Intelligence Methods for Optimization of the Software Testing Process
https://doi.org/10.1016/B978-0-32-391913-5.00021-X

9.2. Exercise 1: Data processing

For solving the exercise in this section you need to review Section 3.3.2. In this exercise, you will practice using Python to load the data from Excel and Word documents and save the data into a variety of formats, while converting and unifying the encoding.

Bonus. Do the same exercises as below, with non–Latin documents. Read about the `str.encode` and `bytes.decode` functions as well as the `python-iconv` package.

1. Load all Microsoft Word files from the provided folder. Save them as UTF-8 encoded text files.
2. Load Excel files into the Pandas data frame and fill in the missing values with respective empties for the column's type.
3. Using regular expressions (regex) and extract and remove the structured portions from the text files generated in the previous point. This makes it possible to separately vectorize the structured portions of the dataset.
4. Given the results of the previous step, tokenize and lemmatize the natural text portions of the files.
5. Remove stop words and all non–alphabetical tokens.
6. Investigate available formats for storing data and their respective advantages and disadvantages. Save the dataset in the following formats: CSV, Pickle, and Feather. How does their speed compare? How easy is it to open them for reading?

9.3. Exercise 2: Natural language processing techniques

For solving the exercise in this section you need to review Chapter 3. As we have noted, measuring the difference between two documents in a natural text can be quite a difficult effort. In this exercise, you will explore some of the approaches with the aim to form a better understanding of when each approach is applicable.

1. Compare different edit distances (Levenshtein distance and Jaccard distance) between the provided files and find the most similar and dissimilar documents. Compare the documents by printing out their contents.
2. Investigate compressibility using gZip of $\frac{1}{4}$, $\frac{1}{2}$, and the full dataset of provided semi-structured data and compare it to the same portions of unstructured text. How does restricted language influence compressibility?

3. Compare different normalized compression distance models by using two of the following compressors: ZlibCompressor, GzipCompressor, DeflateCompressor, with the dataset from the previous exercise.
4. Use the tokenized text from the previous section (Section 9.2) and implement one-hot encoding. How much memory does the final encoded dataset occupy?
5. Based on the tokenized text from Section 9.2, implement TF-IDF encoding.

9.4. Exercise 3: Clustering

For solving the exercise in this section you might need to review Chapter 3. On a number of occasions, it can be useful to employ unsupervised learning methods, specifically clustering to discover the relationships in the input data. In this exercise, you will investigate some clustering methods preparing you for the use of them on real data.

1. Use different clustering algorithms to cluster the provided dataset.
2. Evaluate the implemented clustering methods by comparing the clustering results to the ground truth using the accuracy, precision, recall, and F1-score metrics.
3. Change the dataset by using L1 or L2 normalization and perform again the clustering and evaluation.
4. Use a custom distance metric and redo steps 1 to 3.
5. Split several randomly chosen points from the initial dataset. Perform clustering on the rest of the dataset. Predict the clustering of the points that were split off. How were the results affected by this? Were the points properly clustered? Compare the efficiency of the different clustering approaches.

9.5. Exercise 4: Classification

For solving the exercise in this section you might need to review Chapter 3. When we have the ground truth available, we can often find a classifier that will perform well on the data. In this exercise, you will explore several types of classifiers and compare their performance.

1. Use support vector machine (SVM), multi-layer perceptron, and XG-Boost for classifying the provided dataset. Rerun the code. Do you get the same results? Make the code that will reproduce the same results

whenever it is run (hint: random variables can often be set in the calls to classifiers).
2. Output the confusion matrix and evaluate the performance of the approaches using the F1-score, AUC, ROC, and Cohen's kappa.
3. Change the dataset by using different normalization, and recluster and reevaluate.

9.6. Exercise 5: Imbalanced learning

For solving the exercise in this section you might need to review Section 3.4. Unlike in the previous exercises, the provided dataset will be imbalanced. Thus you might need to take additional steps to prevent the dataset imbalance from negatively affecting the results.
1. Use SVM, multi-layer perceptron, and XGBoost to classify the given dataset and evaluate it using the F1-score, AUC, ROC, and Cohen's kappa.
2. Use oversampling, undersampling, or hybrid sampling method to balance the dataset at ratios of 1.0 and 0.5. Evaluate the results using the F1-score, AUC, ROC, and Cohen's kappa.
3. Use SMOTE to synthesize new data points and thus balance the dataset at ratios of 1.0 and 0.5. Evaluate the results using the F1-score, AUC, ROC, and Cohen's kappa.

9.7. Exercise 6: Dimensionality reduction and visualization

For solving the exercise in this section you might need to review Section 3.5. When working with high-dimensional data, it is often necessary to visualize it in two dimensions. In this exercise, you will explore several approaches for accomplishing this.
1. Load the provided high-dimensional dataset and use principal component analysis to reduce it to two and three dimensions. Plot the results on a 2D and 3D graph.
2. Identify the closest pair and the most distant pair of points using cosine distance. Identify the pairs on the 2D and 3D graphs (for example by drawing a line between them).
3. Use the results from the previous step and cluster the data points using fuzzy C-means. Evaluate the results against the ground truth using the F-score.

4. Use SVM on the 2D data and plot decision regions using the function `plot-decision-regions` from the library `mlxtend.plotting`. Evaluate the effectiveness of SVM using the F-score.

5. Use multidimensional scaling to dimensionally reduce the data to two dimensions. Repeat the previous step and compare the results.

References

[1] A. Robins, J. Rountree, N. Rountree, Learning and teaching programming: A review and discussion, Computer Science Education 13 (2) (2003) 137–172.

Ground truth, data collection, and annotation

A.1. Ground truth

Ground truth refers generally to information that is known to be real, actual, and true, as confirmed by direct observations or measurement [1]. The ground truth can be considered as an opposed term to information that is provided by inference or empirical evidence. In the areas of statistics and machine learning, the ground truth enables the possibility of checking the obtained results of a machine learning model against the real world in terms of accuracy. Having a proper ground truth can help data scientists and researchers employ supervised learning techniques, which can prove or disprove the research hypotheses or the feasibility of a machine learning model. In this chapter, we provide more details regarding the utilized ground truths which have been applied for the performance evaluation of the case studies in Chapter 5. The provided ground truths in this chapter have been derived as follows:

1. analyzing the software architecture,
2. analyzing the testing platforms,
3. employing a compressed annotation matrix,
4. data annotation (data labeling) using several questionnaires and surveys.

Moreover, we attempted to provide general solutions for conducting the ground truths where they can be easily adapted and applied in other cases in industries. The main criterion for the proposed approaches for gathering the labeled data is time efficiency since the main goal of this book is optimization.

A.1.1 The conducted ground truth for Case Study 1, requirements specifications analysis – The Singapore Project at Alstom Sweden AB

Fig. A.1 presents a part of the conducted ground truth analysis for topic identification and clustering presented in Case Study 1 in Section 5.2.2. This information is extracted from the DOORS database at Alstom Sweden

AB, which shows the names of the designed sub-level functional groups for the Singapore R151 project.

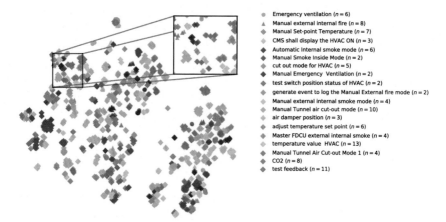

Emergency ventilation ($n = 6$)
Manual external internal fire ($n = 8$)
Manual Set-point Temperature ($n = 7$)
CMS shall display the HVAC ON ($n = 3$)
Automatic Internal smoke mode ($n = 6$)
Manual Smoke Inside Mode ($n = 2$)
cut out mode for HVAC ($n = 5$)
Manual Emergency Ventilation ($n = 2$)
test switch position status of HVAC ($n = 2$)
generate event to log the Manual External fire mode ($n = 2$)
Manual external internal smoke mode ($n = 4$)
Manual Tunnel air cut-out mode ($n = 10$)
air damper position ($n = 3$)
adjust temperature set point ($n = 6$)
Master FDCU external internal smoke ($n = 4$)
temperature value HVAC ($n = 13$)
Manual Tunnel Air Cut-out Mode 1 ($n = 4$)
CO2 ($n = 8$)
test feedback ($n = 11$)

Figure A.1 The corresponding ground truth for requirement vectorization in Case Study 1, presented in Section 5.2.2. The Singapore R151 project at Alstom Sweden AB is utilized for conducting this ground truth analysis.

The presented topics in Fig. A.1 (e.g., emergency ventilation, manual internal-external fire) represent different sub-functions, where the number assigned to each topic shows the number of created requirements for each sub-function. In Case Study 1, the information in Fig. A.1 was hidden from the model and we just utilized the text behind each requirements specification for the vectorization. Later the obtained results have been evaluated against the presented information in Fig. A.1. We need to consider that the provided information in Fig. A.1 is not always available in the testing processes, where applying Case Study 1 can help the testing team to cluster the similar topics among the requirements specification.

A.1.2 The conducted ground truth for Case Study 2, splitting up requirements into dependent and independent classes – The Singapore R151 Project at Alstom Sweden AB

Fig. A.2 shows a segment from the software architecture at Alstom Sweden AB, which has been employed for the dependency detection between requirements for Case Study 2, presented in Section 5.2.4.

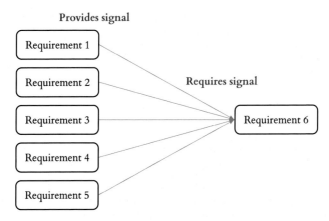

Figure A.2 The corresponding ground truth for requirement vectorization in Case Study 2, presented in Section 5.2.4. This figure shows a segment from the software architecture designed for the Singapore R151 project.

The requirements in the Singapore R151 project are specific to a certain software module and can be seen as a white box. These requirements specify the needs of every individual software module. The links between the requirements in Fig. A.2 show which requirement satisfies a certain function. The dependencies between requirements are indicated in the structure of the Singapore R151 project using "Provides" and "Requires" signals, as can be seen in Fig. A.2.

"Requires signal" represents the required input for a certain requirement, while "Provides signal" represents outputs that influence a requirement. In the provided example in Fig. A.2, Requirement 6 depends on Requirements 1, 2, 3, 4, and 5, due to the "Requires signal," which will be provided by the five other requirements. Moreover, Requirements 1, 2, 3, 4, and 5 are independent requirements in the presented example in Fig. A.2.

Information about the requirements for conducting this ground truth analysis is extracted via analyzing the software architecture. The main objective of proposing a vectorization-based solution for finding the dependencies between the requirements is that the presented information in Fig. A.2 is not always available. On the other hand, analyzing software architecture for each project is a time-consuming process, and the way that the interaction between software modules is designed might differ between different projects. However, the text behind each requirement can be easily extracted from the databases.

A.1.3 The conducted ground truth analysis for Case Study 3, similarity and dependency detection between manual integration test cases – The BR490 Project at Alstom Sweden AB

As stated in Case Study 3, presented in Section 5.3.2, the dependencies between the requirements and also the test cases can be detected by analyzing the signal communications between software modules [2].

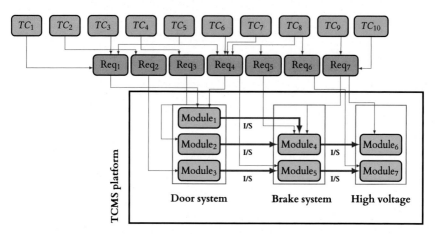

Figure A.3 The corresponding ground truth for test case vectorization in Case Study 3, presented in Section 5.3.2. This figure shows a cut from a testing platform for the BR490 project at Alstom Sweden AB, where the input–output signals, requirements, and test cases are visualized.

Assume that test case TC_2 is functionally dependent on test case TC_1. Then if TC_1 fails during the testing process, TC_2 will fail as well. This kind of dependency has been observed in several cases in different domains [3,4]. Therefore, detecting the dependencies between test cases is important, since it can be utilized later for different test optimization purposes as presented in Case Study 3. In this regard, the structure of the train control management system (TCMS) which is one of the testing platforms at Alstom Sweden AB has been analyzed for conducting this ground truth analysis (see Fig. A.3). As can be seen in Fig. A.3, two test cases are functionally dependent on each other if the output *internal signal* from the corresponding software module enters as an input *internal signal* to another corresponding software module. Indeed, if there exists any shared *internal signal* between two software modules (transmitting and receiving the same *internal signal*), then these two modules are dependent on each other. Thereby, there is a dependency between all requirements and test cases that are assigned to test those software modules. For instance, TC_7 is functionally dependent on TC_2 because an internal signal from **Module$_3$** enters **Module$_5$**. To clarify the presented information in Fig. A.3 from the testing perspective, see Fig. A.4, which shows just the dependent test cases detected by using the provided information in Fig. A.3.

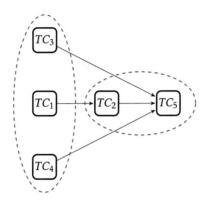

Figure A.4 An example of an embedded directed graph of dependencies for five test cases.

For clustering or classifying test cases based on their dependencies, we can employ their test specifications, as presented in Case Study 3.

A.1.4 The conducted ground truth analysis for Case Study 4, dividing manual integration test cases into dependent and independent classes – The Singapore R151 Project at Alstom Sweden AB

As stated before, the dependencies between test cases can be detected via analyzing the software architecture. However, the way that software architecture is designed differs from project to project, even in the same company. Proof of this claim can be observed in the several ground truth analyses carried out at Alstom Sweden AB.

Fig. A.5 visualizes the conducted ground truth analysis for Case Study 4, presented in Section 5.3.4. As we already reviewed, part of the provided information in Fig. A.5 is already utilized for the dependency detection between requirements in the Singapore R151 project. In Fig. A.5 the designed test cases corresponding to each requirement are added. Moreover, the same hypothesis for dependency detection is used in Case Study 4. In fact, two test cases are dependent on each other if their corresponding re-

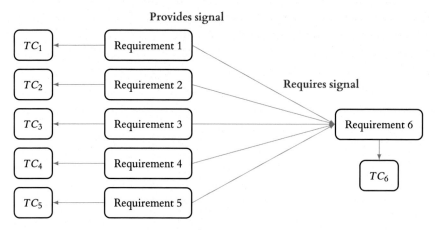

Figure A.5 The corresponding ground truth for test case vectorization for Case Study 4, presented in Section 5.3.4. This figure shows a cut from the software architecture designed for the Singapore R151 project.

quirements share an internal signal. Employing the provided information in Fig. A.5, the one-to-one dependency between all designed test cases for the Singapore R151 project is detected.

Fig. A.6 visualizes the dependencies between requirement and test cases for the Singapore R151 project. In total, 1253 requirements and 668 test cases are utilized in Fig. A.6. Moreover, in total, 2302 edges between requirements and requirements and 1118 edges between test cases and requirements are identified.

Case Study 4 aims to split up all the test cases into dependent and independent classes. Fig. A.7 shows the divided test cases into two main classes using the proposed pipeline for conducting Case Study 4.

In other words, Fig. A.7 shows the output of Case Study 4, where a combination of the text vectorization and classification is employed instead of analyzing the software architecture in Fig. A.5.

A.1.5 The conducted ground truth analysis for Case Study 5 and Case Study 6, similarity detection between integration test scripts – Ericsson AB

In both Case Study 5 and Case Study 6, the similarities between test scripts are considered for applying various optimization approaches. In order to detect the similarities between the utilized test scripts (written in Java language and designed for integration testing), we conducted a survey analysis.

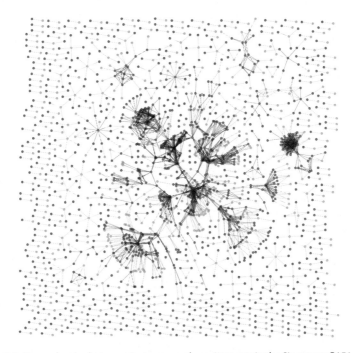

Figure A.6 Dependencies between test cases and requirements in the Singapore R151 project. The red nods represent the requirements and the blue nodes are the test cases.

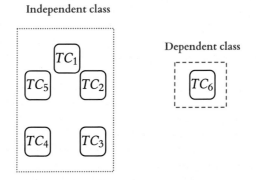

Figure A.7 Classifying test cases into two main classes: dependent and independent.

In this regard, a survey that includes a subset of the test scripts is designed and shared between subject matter experts who are working on different projects at Ericsson AB. A sample of the employed questionnaire is presented in Table A.1.

Table A.1 A sample of the employed questionnaire at Ericsson AB for detecting the similarities between test scripts written in Java. We asked the testers to insert 1 if two test scripts have at least one similar function and insert 0 if there is no similar function between two test scripts.

Tester ID	Test script ID	Binary attributes				
		TC_1	TC_2	TC_3	TC_4	TC_5
	TC_1	1	0	1	0	1
	TC_2	0	1	0	1	0
A	TC_3	1	0	1	1	0
	TC_4	0	1	1	1	0
	TC_5	1	0	0	0	1

As we can see in Table A.1, we asked the testers to insert 1 if two test scripts have at least one similar function and insert 0 if there is no similar function between two test scripts. The testers who participated in this analysis worked for several years with test script generation and test execution. As shown in Table A.1, a binary attribute is specified for each single test script, where each test script is similar to itself. However, it might be the case that the answer from the questionnaires vary from each other since human work and judgment has been employed. To overcome this issue, the majority rule is applied for all three questionnaires.

Fig. A.8 visualizes the conducted ground truth analysis for Case Study 5 and Case Study 6 using the provided information by the testers (part of this information was presented in Table A.1). In fact, Fig. A.8 illustrates the conducted ground truth analysis for similarity detection between test scripts, where the diagonals are removed in Fig. A.8. The filled-in squares in Fig. A.8 indicate that these two test scripts are functionally similar.

A.1.6 The conducted ground truth analysis for Case Study 7 and Case Study 8, grouping log files based on failure causes – Ericsson AB

Excluding the text from each log file, a ground truth for the training set is required as we are using a classification algorithm to address the problem (supervised learning). The ground truth is designed by us using the knowledge provided by the subject matter experts at Ericsson AB. In this regard, we designed several surveys where the subject matter experts are provided a list containing different troubleshooting activities for each failed test case employing their knowledge. In order to decrease human judgment and am-

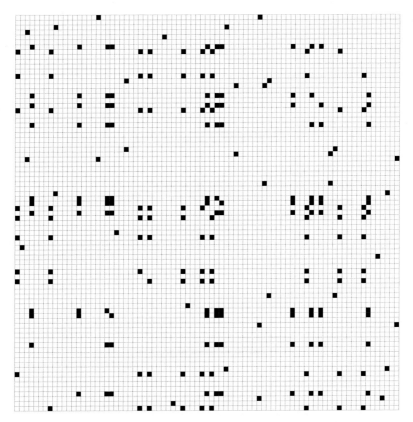

Figure A.8 The corresponding ground truth for similarity detection between test scripts in Case Study 5 and Case Study 6, presented in Section 5.4.2 and Section 5.4.3, respectively. This figure shows a representation of the similarities after the majority-voting across three expert datasets. The filled-in squares indicate that these two test scripts are functionally similar.

Table A.2 A sample of the employed questioner at Ericsson for detecting the failure causes and thereby the required troubleshooting activities.

Tester ID	Log file	Troubleshooting action				
		C_1	C_2	C_3	C_4	C_5
	Log_1	0	1	0	0	1
	Log_2	0	0	1	0	1
B	Log_3	1	0	0	1	0
	Log_4	1	1	0	0	0
	Log_5	0	0	0	1	0

biguity, the designed surveys have been submitted to several subject matter experts. In total, 2368 data points were labeled by subject matter experts.

Employing this information, a ground truth table is constructed, consisting of a matrix containing the test case names and log group as rows and the proper troubleshooting activities as columns (see Table A.2). A test case is marked with 1 in the matrix cell if it is correctly mapped to the troubleshooting activity of that row and 0 otherwise.

References

[1] S. Li, Q. Hao, G. Gao, X. Kang, The effect of ground truth on performance evaluation of hyperspectral image classification, IEEE Transactions on Geoscience and Remote Sensing 56 (12) (2018) 7195–7206.

[2] S. Tahvili, M. Ahlberg, E. Fornander, W. Afzal, M. Saadatmand, M. Bohlin, M. Sarabi, Functional dependency detection for integration test cases, in: 2018 IEEE International Conference on Software Quality, Reliability and Security Companion (QRS-C), 2018, pp. 207–214.

[3] S. Arlt, T. Morciniec, A. Podelski, S. Wagner, If A fails, can B still succeed? Inferring dependencies between test results in automotive system testing, in: 2015 IEEE 8th International Conference on Software Testing, Verification and Validation (ICST), 2015, pp. 1–10.

[4] S. Tahvili, M. Saadatmand, S. Larsson, W. Afzal, M. Bohlin, D. Sundmark, Dynamic integration test selection based on test case dependencies, in: 2016 IEEE Ninth International Conference on Software Testing, Verification and Validation Workshops (ICSTW), 2016, pp. 277–286.

Index

Printed in the United States
by Baker & Taylor Publisher Services